Perfect Points

Contemporary
Hawaiian Appliqué

by Maggie Davies

To Barbara,
Best Wishes
Maggie Davies

TEAMWORK
CRAFTBOOKS

Front cover shows a detail of *Anthurium Wall-Hanging*, 2004
Title page features *French Connection*, 1998

For details of talks and workshops contact Maggie Davies, 8 Lassington Grove, Highnam, Glos GL2 8DA, UK
e-mail: maggiepapercuts@aol.com

Illustrations © Teamwork Craftbooks

First published 2004 by Teamwork Craftbooks

The right of Maggie Davies to be identified as Author of this Work has been asserted by her in accordance with the Copyright, Designs and Patent Act 1988.

The author and publishers can accept no legal responsibility for any consequences arising from the application of information, advice or instructions given in this book. The use of trade names within this book is in no way intended to be an infringement of copyright.

ISBN 0 9532590 7 2
British Library Cataloguing in Publication Data
A catalogue record for this book is available from the British Library

Designed and edited by Christopher and Gail Lawther, Teamwork Craftbooks, 44 Rectory Walk, Sompting, Lancing, West Sussex BN15 0DU

Printed by Sompting Press Ltd
3 The Parade, Cokeham Road, Lancing, West Sussex

FOREWORD

I first met Maggie in the early years of the City & Guilds Course in Patchwork and Quilting; she was an enthusiastic quilter who was keen to study. She came to the course as an already competent craftsperson, studied with enthusiasm, and was always willing to share with her fellow students how she had overcome a problem. Over the years since then I've met her around the UK and on the continent at various quilt shows, willingly passing on her knowledge to others. It was a natural progression for Maggie to become a lecturer and now an author, putting her knowledge and experience into print.

She chose the Hawaiian quilting technique for her final quilt for the City & Guilds certificate.

She made a stunning quilt in black and white (*Broken Images,* below) which no-one could ever forget: a striking tone contrast showing off a beautiful pattern. In this book she passes on to you a true feeling for the subject of Hawaiian quilting. Within its pages you'll find techniques and skills that she has personally evolved, an interesting insight into the history of the Hawaiian quilt – which she gained first-hand from those at the forefront of quilting in the Hawaiian islands – and designs planned to highlight the various skills.

Dinah Travis, *May 2004*

Dinah Travis is known for bringing quiltmaking into education. She·has written several books on quiltmaking and is a practising quiltmaker exhibiting both nationally and internationally.

Broken Images, 1992

William's Garden, 1991

INTRODUCTION

For the past ten years I've been encouraging students to develop their own appliqué skills. During this time I've developed a new method for needle turn appliqué, perfect points and those tiresome inverted Vs. I believe that these methods are fast and easy, but I'll let you be the judge!

As a practical person, I'm always trying to understand why something works well. My aim in this book is to show you just how the technique I've developed for Hawaiian appliqué works, guiding you through every stage with clear text and step by step diagrams. Where relevant I've included separate diagrams for right-handed and left-handed quilters, and throughout the book I've included proven tips which will help you produce successful designs.

I've begun the book with a short précis of the fascinating history of Hawaiian appliqué and quiltmaking. This is followed by the story of my own 'hands-on' research into the subject on the islands themselves. (Hawai`i is made up of a number of islands including Oahu, Maui, Kaui, Moloki, Niihau, Lanai, Kahoolawe, and the big island of Hawai`i. The capital, Honolulu – and Pearl Harbor – are on Oahu.) The technical section comes next, and once you've mastered the basic techniques of needle turn appliqué you can apply them to your own designs, or try out the patterns which I've included in the project section. Finally, if you'd like to take your exploration of Hawaiian appliqué further, you'll find details of additional reading at the end of the book (see page 112).

Whatever your level of experience as a quilter, I hope that this book will encourage you to experiment with the endless possibilities for both traditional and contemporary designs. I hope that you'll join me in perpetuating the truly unique art form known as Hawaiian appliqué.

One small note about the spelling of Hawai`i. In the west we're used to the name appearing as Hawaii, but the way it's spelt by the islanders includes the glottal stop (`) to separate the syllables, so I'll stick to this spelling throughout the book. The glottal stop isn't needed with the word Hawaiian, however – just in case you're wondering!

Maggie Davies

A short history of Hawaiian appliqué

A love of fine bedding

Long before Captain Cook visited the Sandwich Islands in 1778, Hawaiians had been renowned for their skills as craftsmen and women in the arts of canoe-making, feather work, fibre-weaving and bark cloth. The women laboured long hours to produce one of the finest bark cloths in Polynesia. The bark cloth known as *tapa* had many uses, from articles of clothing to a bedding cover known as the *kapa moe*. The Hawaiians valued fine bedding and the women spent many hours making bed coverlets. The thickness of the bedding depended upon your wealth and status, with poorer families settling for less. Each set of *kapa moe* comprised five large white sheets of *tapa* cloth, of a uniform size, with only the top layer dyed and generously decorated with stamp printing.

The *tapa* cloth was made from the *wauke* (or paper mulberry) tree. The men would fell the young trees when the trunk reached between one and two inches in diameter, then the women would peel long, continuous strips of bark from the poles. The green outer bark was separated from the inner bark, most probably with a seashell, and the strips were then placed in water for several days to soften the inner bark, known today as *bast*. Once the bark had softened sufficiently, the strips were then left to dry until a large portion of the water had evaporated and the fibres had begun to stick together. At this stage it was safe to lift the strips from the ground without them breaking into pieces.

Two examples of Hawaiian *Kapa* (barkcloth); the one on the right is made from *wauke*

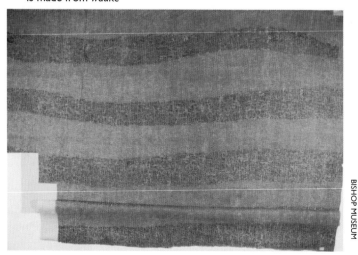

The wet fibre was placed on a *kua kuku* (a flat wooden anvil) and beaten with several different wooden beaters. The makers would then begin the lengthy process of beating, stretching and shaping the surface until the fibres expanded to a uniform size. To obtain larger sheets, strips of *tapa* were joined by overlapping the two edges and beating them until the fibres felted together. Finally the wet *tapa* (or *kapa*) was beaten with an *i`e kuku* (a four-sided decorated wooden mallet) to leave subtle watermarks on the surface before the cloth was placed in the sun to dry. The air and sun-drying turned the cloth white in a short space of time.

The individual stamps were made from a split bamboo cane with designs carved onto the inside surface. The pronged stamps were then dipped into natural dyes and used to decorate the coverlets' top layer, known as the *kilohana*. Unlike today, all of the dyes were obtained from natural sources found on the islands. One such source was the *kukui* tree; this tree alone could yield several different colours ranging from copper red to black. The five layers of

Hawaiian *Kapa* (barkcloth). Material: *wauke*. Watermark: *maka upena pupu*. Use: *kapa pa`u* (skirt).

the *kapa moe* were all held together at the bottom with either stitches or glue. The glue (a diluted starchy mixture called *poi*) was made from the *taro* plant, a staple Hawaiian food and medicine source; the thread was most probably made from *olonā* fibre. To keep the bedding fresh, each set was laundered by washing the surface with a damp cloth before air-drying in the sun. During the day, the bark cloth bedding was rolled away with bits of scented bark, vine or seeds inserted between the layers, and stored in the rafters of the islanders' homes.

The first Hawaiian quilting bee

In the autumn of 1819, a small group of Protestant missionaries and their wives set sail from Boston, New England for the Hawaiian Islands in the Pacific – or, as Mark Twain put it, 'To the loveliest fleet of islands anchored in any ocean.' Finally, after six months at sea, the ship *Thaddeus* anchored off the main island of Hawai`i in the spring of 1820. A scouting party was despatched, shortly returning to announce the death of the monarch Kamehameha the Great and that his eldest son, Liholiho, had been proclaimed king. One of the missionaries' wives, Lucy Thurston, kept a diary in which it was documented that the first meeting with several high-ranking Chiefs took place on the evening of 2 April 1820, not on dry land but on board their vessel. It was during that visit that the dowager queen Kalakua and other royal wives noticed the New England sampler quilts made by the missionaries on the long sea voyage for their new homes. The dowager queen was instrumental in the party's return the very next morning to form the first quilting bee on 3 April 1820. They were all seated on *lauhala* mats on deck. Lucy Thurston noted in her diary that, 'Kalakua, queen dowager, was directress … Mrs Holman and Mrs Ruggles were executive officers, to ply the scissors and prepare the work. The four

women of rank were furnished with calico patchwork to sew, a new employment to them.'

There is no documented evidence of whether the royal party ever completed the patchwork they began on the morning of 3 April. The novelty of stitching was a great success though, and they struck up a mutual friendship with needle and thread. The brightly-coloured geometric patchwork quilts were both practical and functional. Hawaiian women were always at a disadvantage though, because they didn't own scraps of fabric – and they weren't used to cutting up material to piece back into different shapes. To them it seemed both futile and impractical. By 1828 the Hawaiian women were perfecting their own sewing skills in the Mission schools and it wasn't long before the first truly Hawaiian style quilt evolved.

The birth of a new art form

To this day the origins of this unique art form remain a mystery. There's no documented evidence of who started this style of Hawaiian appliqué, and where. Of course there are many delightful stories: I'll briefly outline two and let you be the judge. One version is that the technique started to evolve in 1858 after the birth of an heir apparent, Prince Albert – the first son born to a monarch in 45 years (see page 14). This prompted many women to make covers as gifts for the baby boy. A second story – and the one I most commonly refer to – is that of a native Hawaiian who

Hawaiian quilt in the Bishop Museum Collection with floral vine design along borders and nine floral motifs in centre of quilt, by Martha Heard, 1868

left a sheet on the ground to dry. Returning later that day she noticed that the sun had moved, casting shadows of a tree's leaves onto the surface of the sheet. The woman found the design so striking that she cut out a pattern and appliquéd it to the white sheet. There are several other wonderful stories referred to in Stella Jones' book *Hawaiian Quilts* (see the bibliography on page 112).

Whatever the exact origins of the craft, it's generally believed that this unique art form resulted from an amalgamation of existing styles from other cultures. Lee Wild wrote: 'Although the method of cutting an overall design from a single piece of fabric was unique to Polynesia, the Hawaiians may have developed the technique after seeing small western appliqué designs' – perhaps paper-cut designs from Baltimore quilts! I believe that this is a distinct possibility. To such skilled craftswomen it would seem a most natural progression from making the *kapa moe* to the *kapa lau*, a unique art form known today as Hawaiian appliqué.

Since the art form evolved there have been few changes to the overall designs. The early quilts had slender central motifs which revealed a lot of the background fabric, and *lei* (borders) were rarely included in the design. Borders were incorporated into the design element in the early twentieth century, and today they are an integral part of the pattern. According to the Hawaiian dictionary, the terms *kapa lau* and *kapa `āpana* are interchangeable, with both referring to a quilt with an appliqué design, although each term has its distinct characteristics. The *kapa*

lau has a central design of either four, six or eight identical segments, cut out from a single square of fabric which has been folded into a quarter, a sixth or an eighth to achieve a repeat pattern. The *kapa `āpana* doesn't feature a linked repeat pattern; instead this design consists of up to six separate motifs symmetrically arranged around the quilt's *piko* (centre).

In the beginning some of the designs came from biblical themes (such as *Rose of Sharon*, *Forbidden Fruit*, *King Solomon's Porch*); quilters then designed patterns to commemorate births, marriages and other events – both national and personal – and sometimes incorporating royal insignia. The motif designs were usually symbolic; for instance, the *ulu* (breadfruit) pattern represented growth. It's still believed today that if your first pattern is of the *ulu*, you will continue to design and cut Hawaiian patterns. As with craft traditions in most cultures, there are myths and superstitions surrounding this technique. For instance, it was considered unlucky to have animals or humans depicted on the quilts. On completion of the quilt there was a special ritual to follow to regain your *mana* (spirit) which had gone into the making of the quilt.

Developing the craft

In the early days of Hawaiian appliqué, fabric was in short supply, and it's believed that someone exchanged forty hogs for a bolt of Turkey red fabric. The colour choice was restricted to red, yellow, blue

Hawaiian quilt, circa 1930, in the Bishop Museum collection. Generally referred to as *the Chamberlain Quilt*

Hawaiian quilt pattern called *Fan and Feather Plume of Kaiulani*, made by Mary Ann Kekaula Palaualelo Muller, circa 1917

BISHOP MUSEUM

BISHOP MUSEUM

Tapa beaters (photo by Lee Wild)

Bamboo stamps (photo by Lee Wild)

or green, applied to white sheeting. As Turkey red was the most readily available colour, most quilters used red on a white background. Red motif designs applied to a yellow background were associated with the Hawaiian royal family, denoting their prestigious rank.

The fabric was first washed to ensure it was colour-fast and pre-shrunk before use. In the early days children were delegated to rinse the fabric along the shoreline in the seawater. Traditionally most designs were cut from an eighth fold, although some quilters liked to use the quarter-fold patterns – but all the designs were cut from a single piece of fabric. Less confident designers would make a paper pattern first, while others would use scissors to cut out the pattern from the fabric freehand. Once the cut motif design had been centred on a *kahua* (background sheet), the owner would then sit in the *piko* (centre) to *pa`i* (tack/baste) the motif to the background sheet. More often than not family members and friends would help at this stage, but only the owner was allowed to sit on the quilt. It was normal practice for only one person to do the *humuwili* (overcasting).

The first appliqué stitches used were *humuwili* (overcast or outline stitch), *humu kā* (cross stitch), *wawae moa* (chicken feet), and *humu kaulahao* (chain stitch). Again there is no evidence of when quilters converted to blind stitch. The former stitches can still be seen in Hawaiian work today, but they're referred to as a labour of love and are used as an embellishment after the motif has been appliquéd to the background surface.

The finished appliquéd top was then layered together before quilting. Unlike today, the early stitchers' choice of wadding (batting) was limited to wool, cotton, *pulu* (tree fern) or domestic animal hair. Quilters preferred wool, as it was lighter and didn't bunch up when it was washed. At first quilting was a social event, with groups of family or friends gathered round a large wooden horse (quilting frame). The height of the frame would depend on whether you sat on a chair or on a mat on the floor to quilt. Again, there is no documented evidence of how *kuiki lau* (contour, or echo) quilting evolved. This relief quilting creates a three-dimensional effect on the background surface and is representative of the waves around the islands' shores. Some of the early quilting designs were taken from the New England sampler quilts, and also from the carved patterns on the wooden *tapa* beaters; others were developed from whatever design source had inspired the pattern. The early quilting designs taught by the missionaries were parallel lines, circles and diagonal squares; later quilters began to incorporate patterns such as clamshell, turtle's back, log cabin and cross-hatching. Once the quilt was completed the maker applied a binding to the outside edges, using a colour that matched the motif.

Patterns were jealously guarded (and in some circumstances they still are today). If anyone was caught cheating – using someone else's patterns – they were denounced at local gatherings, or the owner of the design would make up a song denouncing the person surreptitiously. After the quilts were washed, they were hung out to dry inside out; most quilt designs were revealed only after completion and once the pattern was named. To quote Lee Wild, an authority on Hawaiian appliqué quilts, 'The naming of a quilt was a highly personal matter. Some quilts have a meaning expressed with Hawaiian subtlety, some are allegorical, yet others embody a completely private meaning (*kaona*)'. The name, more often than not, did not resemble the design resource, and the meaning remained known only to the individual maker.

Design sources

The Hawaiian quilters took their inspiration from everyday life. The native flora on the islands gave them an abundant design resource to draw on, and sometimes designs were created to celebrate the import of new plants. Early quilt designs included the *ulu* (breadfruit); the *lehua* blossom of the island of Hawai`i; the crown flower – a favourite flower of the last reigning Queen Lili`uokalani; and historical events such as coronations and Halley's Comet. Other favourites were symbols of the *ali`i* (sovereigns), such as the kingdom's coat of arms, the *kahili* (feather standards) with designs dating back as far as 1886, or crowns and fans.

Quilters also took their inspiration from the royal residences on the islands, in particular the `Iolani Palace, completed in 1882 under the rule of King Kalākaua. There are also motifs taken from the palace, including those inspired by the installation of gas lights, the patterns etched in the glass of the front doors, and even the railings; others depict the pavilion constructed for Kalākaua's coronation. Without a doubt the most beloved of all quilt patterns was the *Ku`u Hae Aloha* (meaning 'my beloved flag').

BISHOP MUSEUM

ABOVE: *Ka Uhi Wai O Ka`ala* from the family of Leabert Kuoleiilunalilo O'Sullivan of Kailua, Hawaii
BELOW: Quilt pattern, traditional 1/8 design (photo by Lee Wild)

Lee Wild wrote that 'There was a great resurgence in this special pattern when Queen Lili`uokalani was deposed (against her people's wishes) in 1893 and when the United States annexed the islands in 1898. Although Hawaiian Flag quilts and Coat of Arms quilts appear in a variety of styles, each remains a special reminder of a kingdom that no longer exists.'

Today's quilters have an even greater wealth of design material to draw on. Once you try the basic

BISHOP MUSEUM

Hawaiian flag quilt named *Ku`u Hae Aloha,* in the Bishop Museum collection, circa 1918, made by Wilhemina Eichinger and Mrs Enos, Maui, Hawaii

principles of designing your own Hawaiian-style patterns, you'll realise that design sources are endless, whether your inspiration comes from nature, drawings, facades on buildings, woodcarvings or even an abstract shape developed from a doodle. The possibilities are endless, and the principle of the repeat pattern is very simple, so why not try creating your own motif?

The inspiration for my designs has come from all sorts of resource materials. I find it very helpful to keep a small drawing book close to hand for sketching patterns or jotting down ideas. There's even a sketchpad on my bedside table, as more often than not I think of something just before settling down to sleep. For the projects in the book I've tried to include something for everyone, including patterns for each nation in the British Isles.

A personal journey of discovery

In the spring of 1995, my husband had organised a surprise holiday to Oahu for me to research Hawaiian Appliqué. We left Munich on a bitterly cold, overcast morning for a tropical paradise! The flight took just over eighteen hours and we arrived in Honolulu late the same night; it was a bit of an anti-climax as we stepped off the aircraft and were met with torrential thunderstorms … The journey to our hotel was quite difficult; visibility was poor, and many of the roads were flooded. Eventually we found our accommodation, quickly unpacked and went straight to bed after the long flight, falling asleep listening to the rain lashing against the windowpanes.

Much to our delight, we woke early the next morning to the sound of birds singing. The relentless rain had ceased, and when we opened the windows the gentle sea breezes carried the wonderful fragrant smells of the tropical blossoms into our room, which was bathed in glorious sunshine.

BISHOP MUSEUM

Hawaiian quilt in the Bishop Museum collection, made by Deborah U Kakalia in 1993 to commemorate the 100th anniversary of the overthrow of the Hawaiian Kingdom

Armed only with a telephone number we went in search of the local quilting group. Looking back now, I still can't believe how fortuitous that chance meeting with Sue Zane Williams (the group tutor) was that morning. Once I'd introduced myself and briefly outlined my reasons for visiting the islands, she suggested five other people that I could call. The group made me very welcome and invited me to spend the rest of the morning with them, observing their work, looking through photograph albums of students' work and patterns, and listening to stories relating to the history of Hawaiian appliqué.

That afternoon I started ringing the people on the list. The first call was to Elaine Zinn, who in turn recommended that I contact Lee Wild; Lee, with Elaine, Gussie Bento and Peggie Ehlke, had been closely involved in documentation days of The Hawaiian Quilt Research Project throughout the islands. I couldn't believe my luck! Lee was indeed a fount of all knowledge, and suggested I contacted Toni Hahn and Valerie Free at the Bishop Museum, and Deborah Pope at The Mission House Museum, to arrange private viewings of the collection of Hawaiian quilts held in storage. Also, Lee invited me to come to her house a few days later to see the collection of documented quilt slides she uses for her lectures on the history of Hawaiian appliqué.

Our journey that Wednesday morning through the different residential areas to Lee's house in the town of Kailua gave me an opportunity to view the plant life growing wild along the roadside, and it wasn't difficult for me to see where many quilters got their inspiration from. Plants that we normally buy in garden centres, such as anthurium, orchids, breadfruit, hibiscus and monstera to name but a few, were thriving in their natural habitat. Lee thought that my husband wouldn't be interested in the quilts but suggested that he might like to see a few of the slides before retiring to read the newspaper by the pool; like me, though, he became so absorbed by the slides that the newspaper remained folded on the sun-lounger and he stayed with me for the entire presentation!

In one morning we'd arranged dates and times to visit the Bishop Museum, which houses the Hannah Baker quilt pattern collection, and the Mission House Museum for a private viewing of their historic quilts.

BISHOP MUSEUM

ABOVE: Hawaiian quilt with pikake tuberose pattern made and designed by Hannah Kuumililani Cummings Baker, in the Bishop Museum collection

RIGHT, TOP: Tuberose plant (photo by Lee Wild)

RIGHT, BELOW: Monstera plant (photo by Lee Wild)

We'd also arranged for me to attend two popular classes, one run by Kepola U. Kakalia (affectionately known by her students as Auntie Debbie), and one by Althea Serrao and her husband John. Armed with all this information we decided to allocate our mornings to research, with most of our afternoons free for sightseeing (and, of course, for visiting different beaches along the coastline).

Our first visit was to the Mission House Museum, located by the Kawaiaha`o Church in the old part of Honolulu. We hoped this would give us an insight into the everyday lives of the early missionaries. The white-framed building was pre-fabricated, shipped from New England around Cape Horn and constructed on site. Today the building is a registered national historical landmark, and houses a unique collection of historical quilts made on the island. During my private viewing I saw one of the oldest and best preserved examples of chicken-feet appliqué stitch, and was amazed at the freshness and brightness of the blue motif fabric. All the quilts were well preserved thanks to the museum's practice of protecting them in a climate-controlled environment.

The Bishop Museum, located in the city centre, was founded by Charles Reed Bishop in honour of his late wife Princess Bernice Pauahi Bishop, the last descendant of the royal Kamehameha family.

Today the museum houses the cultural artefacts of the Hawaiian and other Pacific Islands. The museum has an interesting display of Hawaiian appliqué quilts, drawn from its extensive collection and displayed on a rotation basis. Through the courtesy of a private viewing I was able to study the museum's quilt collection, in particular the pikake tuberose quilt (above), designed and made

Hawaiian quilt with blue lily appliqué on white background, in the Bishop Museum collection

ABOVE: Hawaiian quilt made by Kauhine Kamalau, 1900.
BELOW: Torch ginger plant (photo by Lee Wild)

by Hannah Baker. Hannah was a well-known tutor and prolific collector of Hawaiian appliqué patterns, which were bequeathed to the museum. At this museum I was also fortunate enough to attend Debbie Kakalia's class on traditional Hawaiian appliqué.

Queen Emma Summer Palace was restored to its former grandeur of the 1870s and administered by the Daughters of Hawai`i. Since 1915 it has housed pictures of the Hawaiian royal family and items of furniture and china from the royal household collection. In particular there are several portraits of the heir apparent Prince Albert, the first son born to the monarch in 45 years; it's believed that the unique Hawaiian appliqué method was first used in quilts made to commemorate his birth in 1858. The museum has its own collection of quilts, but only displays one at a time on public view.

The following week I spent a wonderful day at a class run in the grounds of the Summer Palace by Althea and John Serrao, learning some of the skills and history of Hawaiian appliqué. In particular, I was fascinated to hear the story of Althea's grandmother Caroline Kealamaihiki Speckman Correa, who encouraged her as a child to learn the history and stories of Hawaiian quilts as well as the stories pertaining to the quilt designs. During the day I was told the story of an embellishment stitch I'd seen on early quilts. Apparently, this was one of the first appliqué stitches, known as *wawae moa* or chicken's feet (see page 52), which was used before blind stitch. This unique husband and wife partnership proudly

shares their knowledge and continues to encourage other quilters to perpetuate this truly unique art form. For me, this story is made even more remarkable as Althea was born with only one hand. I think this should be an inspiration to us all!

The Waianae Library houses a collection of quilt patterns, started by Hannah Perry, which now exceeds over four hundred patterns. The library is well worth a visit as you're permitted to trace the patterns provided that you supply your own tracing materials.

I left the island feeling overwhelmed by the generosity, help and kindness shown to me during my all-too-brief stay. My research had well exceeded my expectations for the visit, and fuelled me with inspiration to design my own work while perpetuating this unique art form.

Materials and equipment

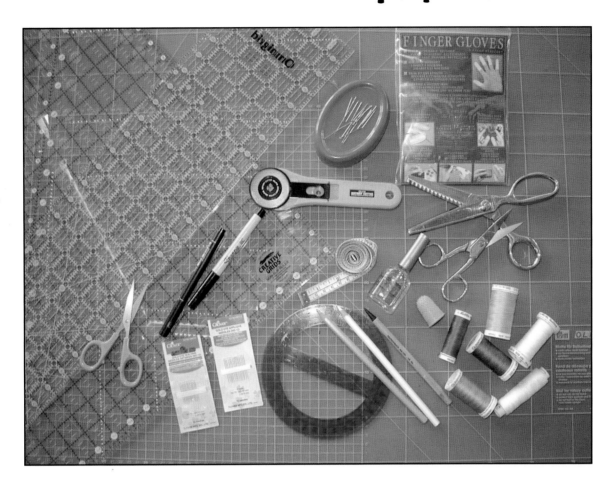

Fabric

For all the projects in this book I recommend 100% cotton fabric. I prefer not to wash my material before I cut the pattern as the fabric sizing helps to maintain a sharp thumbnail-creased edge. Most fabrics today don't need washing, but if you're at all in doubt do pre-wash; I strongly recommend that you then use a spray starch to renew the fabric sizing before working on your appliqué.

> **TIP** *Cut a small square of the motif fabric, and drop it straight into boiling water; you'll be able to see straight away if any colour leaches out. If the fabric is colour-fast there's no need to pre-wash it.*

There's no reason why you can't use most of the fabrics available today for this technique; I do suggest that you do a little trial piece first, though, to see how the fabric works when it's appliquéd. With some fabrics you may find that you need to add a larger turning allowance to accommodate their different weaves – this will be an important factor when you're designing your motif.

If you've done any Hawaiian appliqué or other detailed appliqué, I'm sure that, like me, you've often wondered why one side of the appliqué motif is easier to handle than the other! The answer simply lies in the warp and weft of the fabric. The warp (selvedge edge) remains taut while the weft (the crossways weave) has greater flexibility. As a result, the two warp sides of the appliqué motif's edges will require more clipping on the straight grain of the fabric, while the two weft sides of the appliqué edges can usually be manipulated without extra clipping.

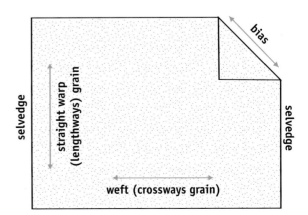

Cutting mat and rotary cutter

There are various sizes and brands of self-healing cutting mats, rotary cutters and safety rulers on the market today; choose the size most suited to you. Remember that the rotary cutter is a very sharp tool and should be used with caution. Always cut away from you, and remember to apply the safety sheath after use.

Non-slip ruler and square

Both these tools are particularly helpful for cutting out, squaring off fabric and trimming the outside edges to the required size after quilting.

Thimbles

There are a host of different thimbles on the market ranging from leather to metal finish. Whether you wear one is a very individual choice; personally, I like to wear the new 'finger gloves' for appliquéing. This does help to prevent those indentations from appearing on your middle finger … I have arthritic joints, and I prefer to use a bankers' thimble for quilting; try different types, and see which you like best.

Threads

For appliqué, use a cotton or cotton-wrapped polyester to match the motif fabric and a white tacking (basting) thread. If you're making up your project by machine, select a thread that matches the background fabric. For quilting, special quilting thread comes in a variety of colours and is much stronger than regular cotton.

Needles

There are special needles for appliqué, often referred to as 'sharps'. These needles are longer than ordinary needles, and the extra length helps you to sculpt the fabric edge under without having to use your fingers. Sharps range in size from number 9 to 12; the higher the number, the finer the needle. For quilting many people prefer a shorter, specialised quilting needle; these are stronger than appliqué needles and will go through three layers of material. Again the sizes range from number 9 to 12; if you're not sure which size to use, select one with the same number as your appliqué needle. I prefer to use Clover Gold Eye Needles for their durability.

Scissors

You'll need a sharp pair of pointed fabric scissors to cut through a maximum of eight layers at one time. My recommendation is Gingher 5in tailor-point scissors, now available from quilting outlets. *Never* use your fabric scissors for cutting out paper; it's a good idea to keep a sharp pair of paper scissors in your basic sewing kit, for use on the paper trials and for cutting out cardboard templates.

Fabric markers

This again is a personal choice; there are many different types of fabric marker on the market. The white and yellow cloth-marking pencils are ideal for tracing outlines onto any coloured fabric. If you need to mark the contour lines onto your background fabric a dry sliver of soap works well.

TIP *I always keep my fabric marking pencils in the freezer when not in use. This helps to maintain a sharp point and prevents waste when sharpening the pencil before use.*

Basic sewing kit

Tacking needles, ordinary straight pins, a small sharp pair of fabric scissors, tape measure.

Other equipment

Other bits of equipment that you'll find invaluable are: an HB propelling (automatic) pencil, broadsheet newspaper, poster cardboard, a protractor, a set of compasses, a sewing machine, a steam iron and ironing board, a plastic triangle, and extra-strength clear nail varnish.

TIP *I apply two coats of clear nail varnish to the skin around the nail on my left index finger before I begin appliquéing. This helps to prevent rough and sore areas from developing while I'm stitching.*

Quilting frames

Once again, the decision to use a frame or not is very much a personal choice. I can't do any hand quilting without a frame, and my preference is for the square plastic frame with extensions for larger projects. Frames of all kinds come in a variety of different sizes, so select the type and size best suited to the projects you'll be doing.

Colour

In the early 1800s the choice of colours was restricted to the availability of imported fabrics. The Hawaiian women used solid colours of red, blue, yellow or green for their motif design, applied to white sheeting. Then, as now, great emphasis was placed on contrasting colours to emphasise the bold appliqué designs.

Lee Wild writes: 'In the early 1880s, turkey red (named after the country, not the fowl) was the most common Western fabric available in Hawai`i, and many early quilts incorporated a red-on-white colour scheme. Some have suggested that the origin of this combination of colours was the red-on-white *pa`i`ula* cover sheet seen on many *kapa moe*. As new fabrics became available, such as chintzes, calicoes and dotted swiss, they were incorporated into this evolving art form.'

With an increasing variety of imported fabrics available, Hawaiian quilters soon began to explore the possibilities of using a third and fourth colour, sometimes to accentuate a certain part of the motif design or add realism to plant forms.

Today, quilters choose a variety of colour combinations, ranging from the traditional through to complementary colours; a printed fabric on a solid colour; and solid or designer fabrics on a dark background. Whatever combination you choose, just as with the very earliest designs, a strong contrast of colours or tones between the motif fabric and the background fabric is the most effective. For this reason, the traditional use of two colours remains extremely popular on the islands.

If you're at all uncertain over your choice of colours, experiment with several small squares of fabric; lay them out in various combinations until you're satisfied with the colour plan.

Hawaiian Doodles, 1996

Pattern layout

Today's quilters are developing new pattern layouts for the traditional and contemporary folds; in this section, I'll explain some of the different pattern layouts that you might like to consider for your own work.

One-eighth (1/8) folds

Traditionally, most patterns were designed for the one-eighth fold with the longest side of the pattern drawn onto the diagonal (bias) line and the shortest side of the pattern drawn onto the straight (vertical) line of the right-angled triangle (**A**).

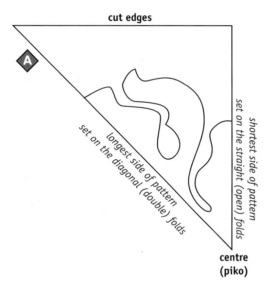

cut edges

A

longest side of pattern
set on the diagonal (double) folds

shortest side of pattern
set on the straight (open) folds

centre
(piko)

When it's cut out and unfolded, this design forms a square-shaped image (**B**). However, there are at least four other pattern layouts to consider.

B

First of all, what happens if you set the same design on point, drawing the longest side of the pattern on the straight (vertical) line and the shortest side on the diagonal (bias) line (**C**)?

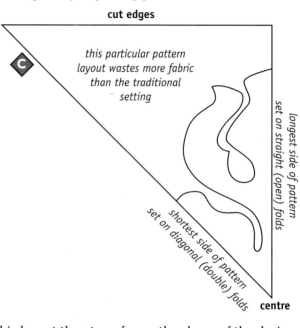

cut edges

C

this particular pattern
layout wastes more fabric
than the traditional
setting

longest side of pattern
set on straight (open) folds

shortest side of pattern
set on diagonal (double) folds

centre

This layout then transforms the shape of the design to a cross- or star-shaped image (**D**), and it will require a much larger background square than the traditional setting.

D

the layout shown
here creates a
cross-shaped or
star-shaped motif

Secondly, if you draw the main features of the pattern into the negative space (the main body of the triangular shape) it will create the optical illusion of a circular pattern on a square background. For this pattern to work you need to have connectors on the straight and diagonal folds (**E** and **F**).

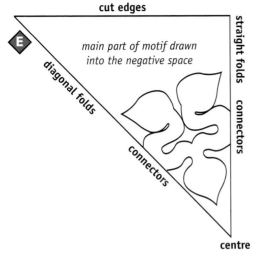

main part of motif drawn into the negative space

cut edges — straight folds — diagonal folds — connectors — connectors — centre

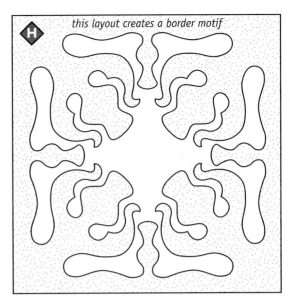

this layout creates a border motif

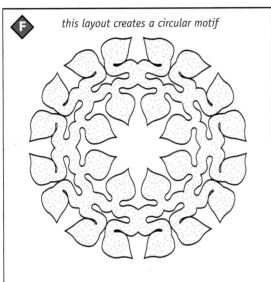

this layout creates a circular motif

Finally, you could consider designing a lei pattern with a negative space above and below the motif (**I**). This type of design can look simple yet elegant (**J**), with a greater emphasis on the contour quilting. You'll find detailed instructions for creating a 1/8 design on page 26.

Thirdly, you can create a border pattern by working the motif design from the outside edge inwards. Just as before you'll need to have connectors on the diagonal and straight folds (**G**). This particular layout leaves a negative space in the centre of the background fabric, focusing more on the contour quilting (**H**).

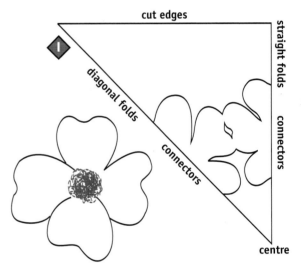

cut edges — straight folds — diagonal folds — connectors — connectors — centre

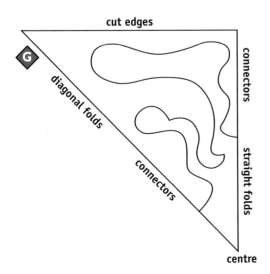

cut edges — connectors — diagonal folds — straight folds — connectors — centre

a simple lei design

One-quarter (1/4) folds

It's still a mystery whether this particular style is unique to Hawai'i or if it evolved from the *Tifaifai* one-quarter designs in the Society Islands. The *Tifaifai* appliquéd quilts consist of two layers (appliquéd top and backing), whereas the Hawaiian quilts have three layers (appliquéd top, wadding and backing).

As with the one-eighth fold you have several options for your pattern layout. First, the traditional layout of your pattern would be from the *piko* (centre) out. This can be particularly useful if the motif form is not symmetrical, or if you want to create an irregular-shaped leaf or flower (**A** and **B**).

Secondly, you could design the pattern from the outside edge in. This again creates interesting negative spaces in the centre of your work, with the contour quilting creating an optical illusion of a raised motif (**C** and **D**).

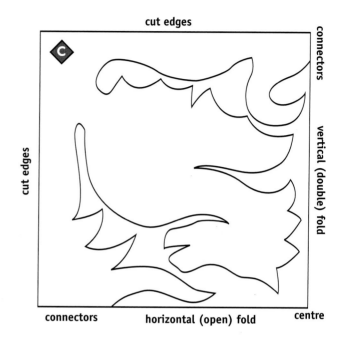

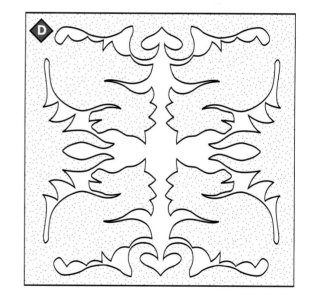

Finally, there is of course another possibility! You could consider working the pattern along the straight of the folds and the outside edge – this creates a series of negative spaces in each quadrant (**E** and **F**). Detailed instructions for creating a 1/4 fold are on page 35.

One-sixth (1/6) folds

The one-sixth fold creates alternative options for pattern layouts on circular, square or hexagonal backgrounds. The exact folding method varies slightly for the different background settings, but the outcome of each is the same: a six-sided motif.

The most common way of designing a pattern for a circular background – a motif which appears to be circular itself – is from the centre out; there are two choices for the motif placement. You can either set the main part of the motif design along the diagonal folds (**A** and **B**), or use them to fill the negative space (**C** and **D,** overleaf), with the smaller parts of the design as the connectors.

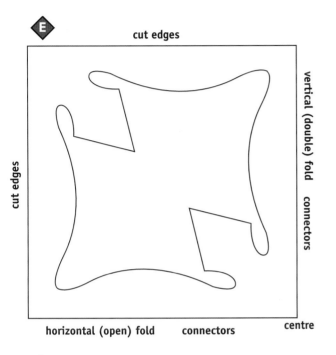

E
cut edges
vertical (double) fold   connectors
cut edges
horizontal (open) fold   connectors   centre

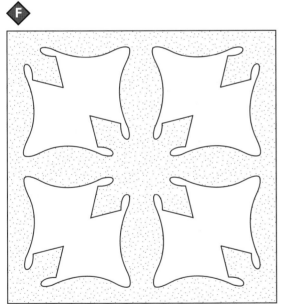

F

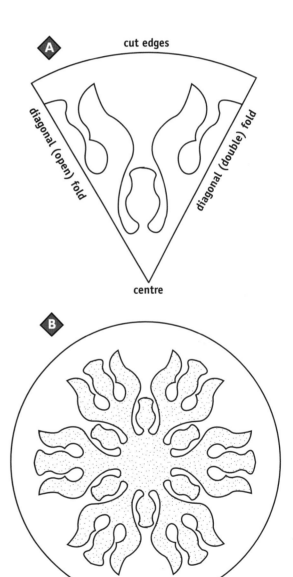

A
cut edges
diagonal (open) fold
diagonal (double) fold
centre

B

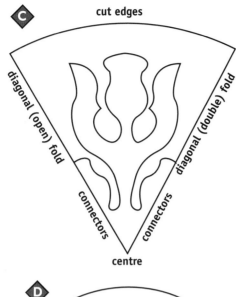

to a filigree motif design for a Christmas tree skirt (**G** and **H**), or even a tier of separate lei patterns (**I** and **J**).

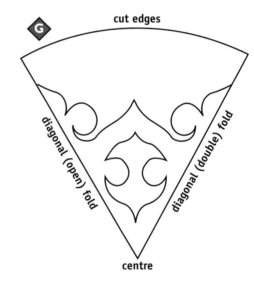

But what if you design your pattern from the outside edge inwards? The design element can be anything from a simple shallow border on a circular tablecloth (for instance the dolphin design shown in **E** and **F**),

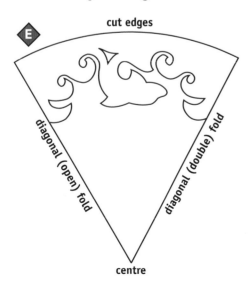

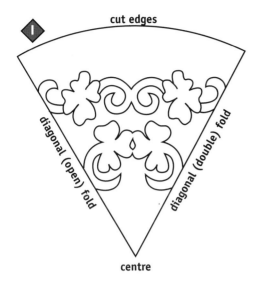

I

cut edges

diagonal (open) fold

diagonal (double) fold

centre

J

Sequence K

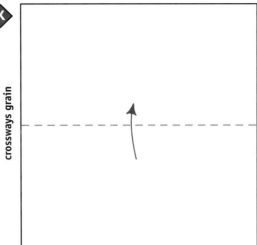

K

lengthways grain

crossways grain

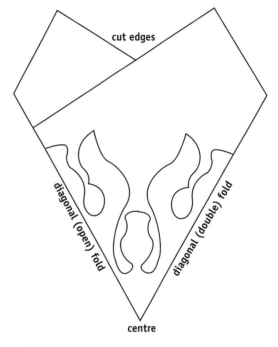

cut edges

diagonal (open) fold

diagonal (double) fold

centre

If you want to design a one-sixth motif for placement onto a square background you'll need to fold the fabric horizontally (sequence **K,** shown right), vertically (sequence **L**, overleaf) or diagonally (sequence **M**, overleaf) before you divide it into equal sections. Once again you have two choices for the pattern layout. The designs will look slightly different, with the first one on point, while the other two are canted to the left or right of the vertical.

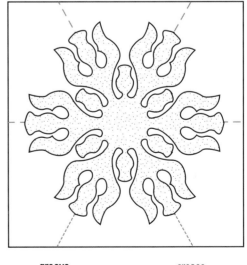

- - - groove   ∨   ········· crease   ∧

Sequence L

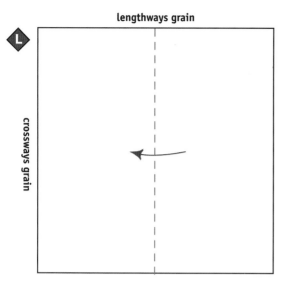

lengthways grain

crossways grain

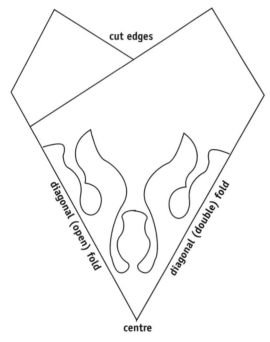

cut edges

diagonal (open) fold

diagonal (double) fold

centre

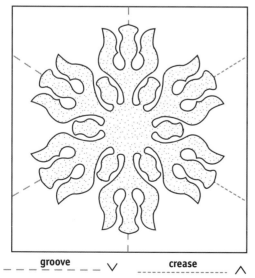

groove ⌄   crease ⌃

Sequence M

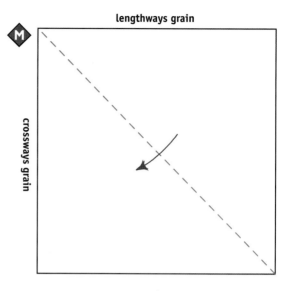

lengthways grain

crossways grain

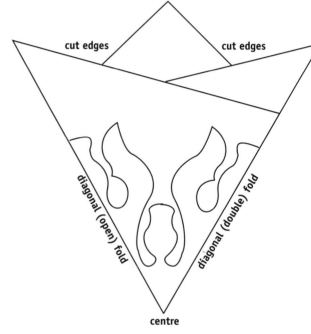

cut edges   cut edges

diagonal (open) fold

diagonal (double) fold

centre

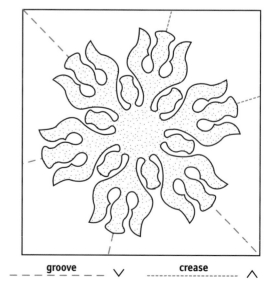

groove ⌄   crease ⌃

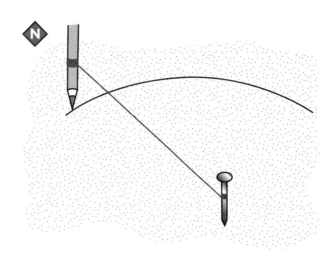

Whether the design is for a circular, hexagonal or square setting you'll need to use a protractor to mark the 60° angles onto the folded fabric. For larger circular projects I've found it particularly helpful to use a compass tool (a large set of compasses) to mark an arch on the outside edge of the folded background fabric, and on the motif fabric for outside edge patterns. If you haven't got a compass tool you can achieve the same results by creating your own version with a short pencil, a length of fine string and a strong quilters' pin or two-inch nail (**N**). You'll find detailed instructions for creating a 1/6 fold on page 37.

These samples demonstrate how I've taken a design from nature and stylised it so that it's suitable for Hawaiian appliqué. Starting with a selection of oak leaves (**A**), I've then sketched several variations of leaf and acorn shapes (**B**). In diagram **C** I've simplified the basic leaf shape so that it fits into a rough triangle, and for the final template (**D**) I've added an acorn shape on the outside and inside. Diagram **E** shows the final design, *Mighty Oak*.

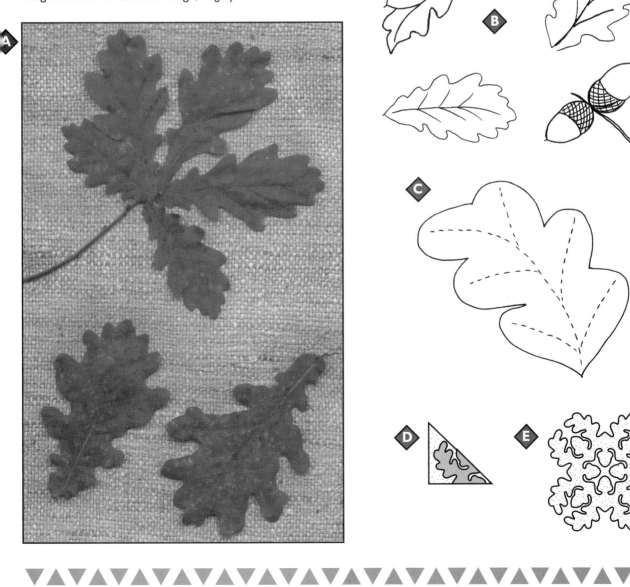

Preparation

Designing a pattern

Before you begin any Hawaiian appliqué projects there are three specific guidelines that you need to take into consideration. First, determine the size of the project; secondly, the shape of the motif; and thirdly, the pattern layout.

For me this is the most exciting part of Hawaiian appliqué – designing, folding and cutting out paper shapes. You have so many possibilities for the pattern layout, and it's only by trial and error that you discover – sometimes by accident – which you like the best!

> **TIP** *I strongly recommend that you do all your pattern trials on paper first. Mistakes do happen, and it can become quite expensive cutting straight on to fabric.*

Pattern cutting

I'm sure we can all remember cutting out snowflakes or paper-chains of little boys and girls from folded paper when we were at primary school! The technique for designing and then cutting out a Hawaiian appliqué pattern uses exactly the same principle. While you're experimenting with the shape and size of the motif and pattern layout, work all of the trials on folded paper rather than cutting directly into fabric.

To demonstrate how the technique works in practice, I'll show you how to design a pattern for an 18in (46cm) cushion cover; for this exercise, we'll use a traditional eighth (1/8) fold – a design which consists of eight segments. I'll then show you how to create a template and cut and prepare the motif ready for appliqué. Most of the basic techniques for cutting and positioning motifs are the same or very similar for quarter (1/4) folds and sixth (1/6) folds, with just a few variations in how the paper and fabric are folded, cut and positioned; I'll explain the variations for these designs in detail on pages 35 and 37.

> **TIP** *The cheapest material for cutting patterns smaller than about 23in (58cm) is a broadsheet newspaper. For larger patterns, the thinnest brown parcel paper can be stuck together with sticky tape and is ideal for folding into multiple thicknesses.*

1 As a rule, the motif is generally designed 2in (5cm) smaller than the finished cushion size, so begin by cutting several 16in (41cm) squares of newspaper.

2 To produce an eighth fold you'll be folding the square of paper three times; the most important part of this process is always to be accurate and consistent in the way you fold. Place one of your squares of paper on a flat surface. First, fold the paper in half horizontally (**A**), then fold the paper in half again vertically to form a quarter fold (**B**).

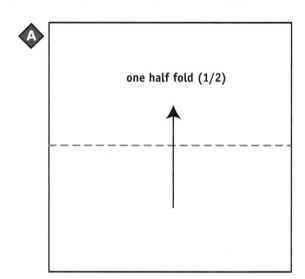

A — one half fold (1/2)

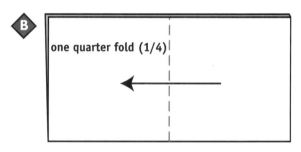

B — one quarter fold (1/4)

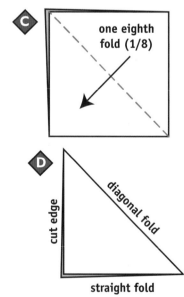

C — one eighth fold (1/8)

D — cut edge / diagonal fold / straight fold

Finally, fold the paper diagonally into an eighth fold (**C**). Finger-press each new fold.

It's vital to pay particular attention when you're doing the third fold; the diagonal and straight folds must meet at the centre point (**D**) to enable you to create a symmetrical pattern.

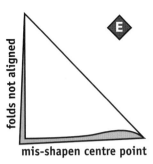

folds not aligned

E

mis-shapen centre point

If this fold isn't accurate, for instance as shown in **E**, the design element can become mis-shapen; this will only become evident after you've cut out the paper pattern – the different parts of the motif won't be symmetrical or of a uniform size.

3 The paper square has now been folded into a right-angled triangle. Before you outline your motif onto this triangle, draw around the shape onto a piece of template cardboard. You may need to straighten the diagonal and straight pencil lines before cutting out the right-angled triangle cardboard replica. Label the diagonal and straight lines on the appropriate edges of the cardboard template (**F**), then set aside the cardboard shape and work on the folded paper.

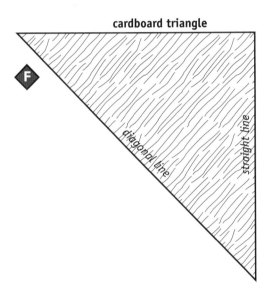

cardboard triangle

F

diagonal line

straight line

TIP *For smaller projects, the cheapest template material is something you've probably got lying around the house – the front and back of a cereal box. For larger designs, buy an A2 sheet of poster card; you can generally get these from art shops or suppliers of office materials.*

4 Once you've decided on the motif shape and pattern layout (see page 18), draw the full-size motif onto the front surface of the folded paper triangle (**G**). Using a pair of sharp paper scissors, cut along the marked lines (**H**) to produce the folded motif shape (**I**), then unfold it and see how it looks (**J**). Don't be too disappointed if the design doesn't work the first time; sometimes it takes several attempts before you're satisfied with the final pattern.

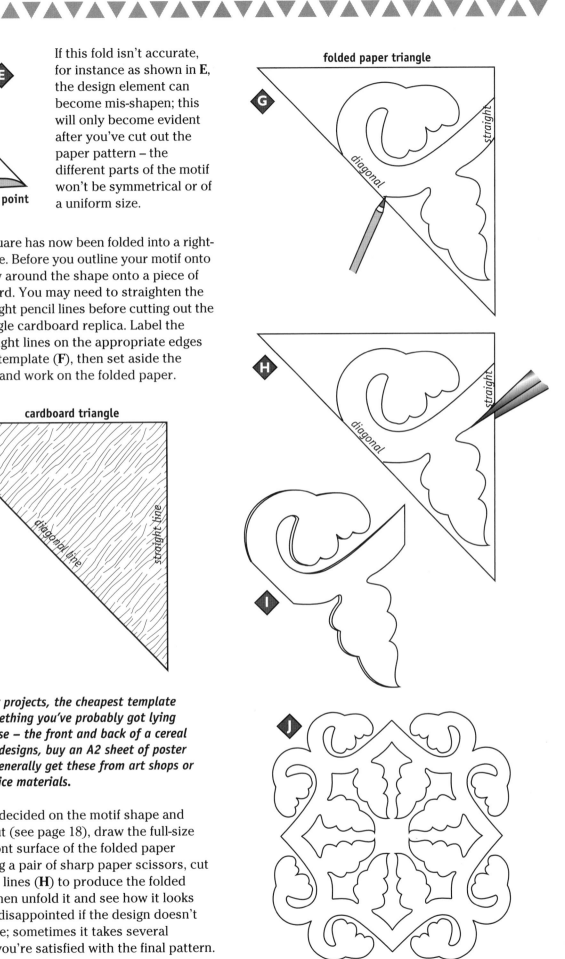

folded paper triangle

G

diagonal

straight

H

diagonal

straight

I

J

TIP *Remember that the motif shape will need 'connectors' on the folded edges to achieve a repeat design (K); if you don't have these connecting parts of the design, for instance in the design show in L, you'll end up with eight individual motif shapes (M).*

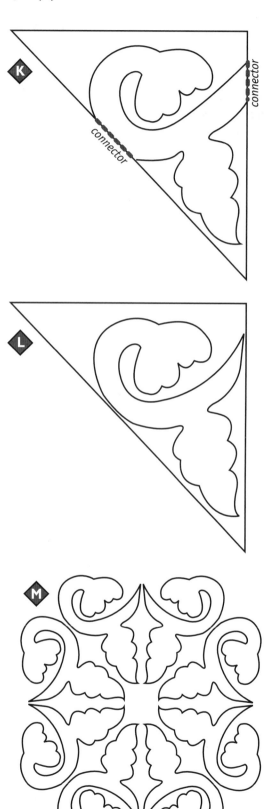

Making a template

1 When the design element works well and the unfolded pattern is to your liking, refold the pattern back into the one-eighth design. Place this paper pattern onto the right-angled cardboard template, matching the diagonal and straight folds of the motif and the cardboard edges. Hold the pattern firmly in place with one hand while you use the other hand to trace around the motif with an HB pencil

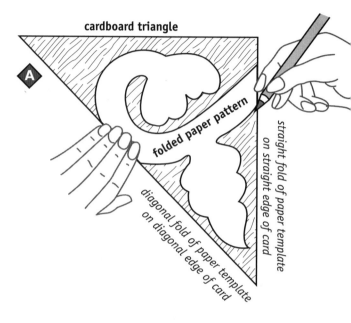

cardboard triangle

folded paper pattern

straight fold of paper template on straight edge of card

diagonal fold of paper template on diagonal edge of card

2 There are two different ways of adding a turning allowance onto a pattern. Either, incorporate the ⅛in (3mm) turning allowance into the shape marked on the cardboard template (**B**); or, before cutting out the motif design, add an ⅛in (3mm) turning allowance to the pencil outline on the fabric surface (**C**).

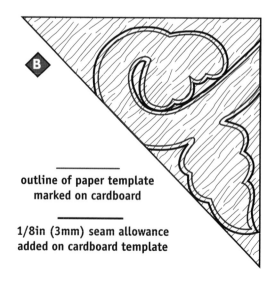

—————
outline of paper template marked on cardboard

—————
1/8in (3mm) seam allowance added on cardboard template

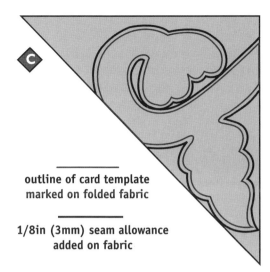

outline of card template marked on folded fabric

1/8in (3mm) seam allowance added on fabric

Personally, I prefer to add the turning allowance to the cardboard template; this prevents any mistakes from happening inadvertently while you're cutting out the motif fabric.

> **TIP** *Remember to add the seam allowance to every edge of the motif, not just the outside line.*

Cutting the fabric

Only when you're totally satisfied with the design elements should you begin to consider cutting out any fabric. Remember, the cut pattern won't resemble the initial motif design very closely, as many of the edges will appear to be connected. The correct shape will only begin to emerge once the motif edges are turned under.

You'll need to cut the background fabric larger than the finished size plus the normal ¼in (6mm) seam allowance. For instance, to make an 18in (46cm) cushion you will need two 19½in (49.5cm) squares; this size provides a ¾in (2cm) seam allowance on all sides. Why do you need all this extra? There are at least three reasons.

- First of all, the background fabric edges tend to fray when continually handled during appliqué.

- Secondly, once a block has been quilted its outside edge has sometimes become mis-shapen; if that happens it will need trimming before you construct the cushion cover, so it's helpful to have some extra built in.

- Thirdly, the extra seam allowance gives you various options on how to construct the edges of the cushion cover – for example, you might choose to finish the edge with a piped cord.

There are many different ways of cutting out fabric. The method you choose isn't important; what **is** important, however, is that your squares are identical

in size if you want to use both the positive and negative shapes cut from one piece of motif fabric (**A**). The shape cut from the centre of the design is the positive (**B**); the shape left round the edge of the folded square is the negative shape (**C**). If you'd like to use a negative (border) shape for an appliquéd motif, you might find it necessary to redefine certain parts of the cut edges (**D**).

However, if you only want to use the positive shape of the design, there's a simple calculation which will help you to estimate the fabric yardage accurately. For this method, it's much easier to measure the straight edge of the cardboard shape before cutting out the motif design (**E**).

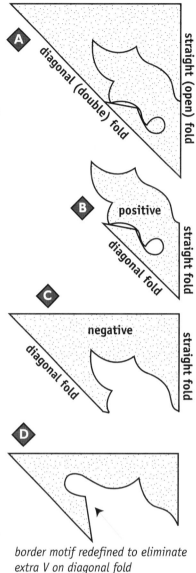

border motif redefined to eliminate extra V on diagonal fold

double measurement between A and B, then add 1/2in (12mm)

This method applies to all designs, even if the centre has been cut away, as in the design shown in **F** – and working on the card template means that you're less likely to forget the central part of the square and measure incorrectly on designs with a central aperture.

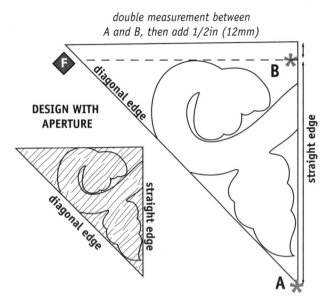

double measurement between A and B, then add 1/2in (12mm)

DESIGN WITH APERTURE

(The only exception to this method of calculation is mentioned in the TIP box below.) Measure from the centre (point A) along the straight line of the cardboard edge to the final outer pencil mark of the motif design (point B). Double the measurement, and then add ½in (12mm) to the overall size of the motif fabric only.

TIP *There's only one exception to the measurement method above: it doesn't apply to any designs beginning from the outside edge inwards (for example see the dolphin circular tablecloth design on page 76).*

Folding the fabric

Always be consistent in the sequence of folding the fabric for the lengthways and crossways grains to correspond. Instead of finger pressing the creases you will need to use a steam iron for each new fold.

1 The choice is yours – positive and negative shapes or just the positive shape! To obtain a positive and negative shape, cut one 19½in (49.5cm) square of background fabric and an identical square of motif fabric. If you are creating a design using the positive shape only, cut one 19½in (49.5cm) square of background fabric and a smaller square of your motif fabric (follow the instructions above to work out the size of the square).

2 When you come to position the motif (see page 32), it will be much simpler and more accurate if you've folded both your squares of fabric in exactly the same way. To prevent any mistakes occurring, place the background and motif fabric squares side by side, right sides up, with the grains corresponding, on the flat surface of your ironing board (**A**); this way you can fold both pieces of fabric in the same way at each stage. It's essential that the grains on the cut squares remain in the same direction; this prevents distortion of the background fabric and the turned appliqué edge.

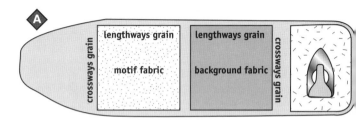

3 For a one-eighth design the fabric will be folded three times. First, fold each of the two squares of fabric in half, right sides together, with the cut edges at the top; carefully press these first horizontal folds with a steam iron (**B**).

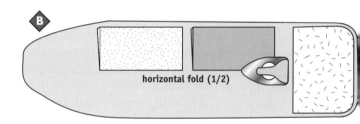

TIP *Let the steam iron glide over the surface rather than dragging the fabric out of shape.*

4 Next, fold each piece of fabric in half again, right to left, matching the corners, to create a quarter fold. Carefully press along the new vertical fold on both pieces of fabric; start pressing from the outside cut edge and work inwards to the centre point (**C**).

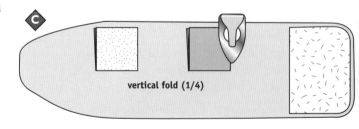

5 Finally, fold each piece of fabric in half again, this time diagonally from right to left (**D**), to create a right-angled triangle (**E**).

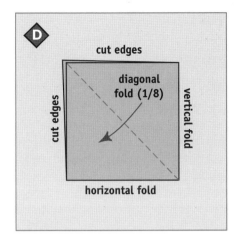

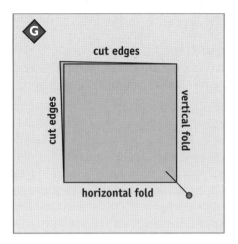

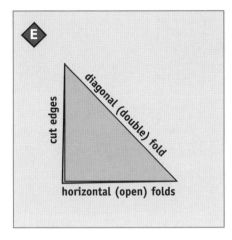

Press along these third (and final) folds, starting from the outside cut edge; slowly and gently let the steam iron glide along the fabric surface from the cut edge, along the diagonal and straight folds towards the centre point (**F**). Using this method for the pressing keeps all the folds equal, and will prevent any fabric distortion around the centre folds.

6 Put the background fabric to one side and work on the folded motif fabric only. This next step is very important and will prevent any of the layers from shifting while you're cutting out the motif pattern. With a large threaded tacking needle, begin tacking from the centre out, stitching through all layers of fabric along the diagonal and straight folds, as close to the folded edges as possible (**H**). Then, run a line of tacking stitches through the centre of the right-angled triangle from the centre point to the outside cut edge (**I**). Depending on the intricacy of your design you may need to add another two horizontal lines of tacking stitches. Your fabric is now ready for marking and cutting.

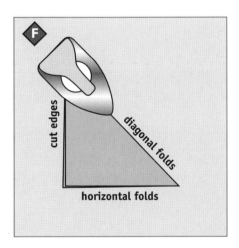

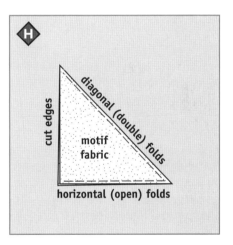

TIP *To help you create an accurate one eighth fold, put a pin diagonally into the bottom right-hand corner of the motif, through all the fabric layers and into the surface of the ironing board, and fold the fabric over the pin from right to left (**G**).*

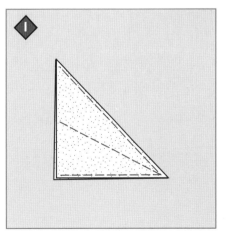

Preparing a design for stitching

Marking and cutting the motif

1 Still working on the motif fabric only, place the cardboard motif template on the fabric surface, aligning the diagonal and straight lines with the diagonal and straight folds of the fabric. Hold the template quite firmly with one hand, and with an HB propelling pencil mark around the outline of the motif (**A**). Be careful not to drag the pencil on the fabric surface as this can also distort the folded layers. Once the motif outline has been drawn onto the fabric surface, remove the cardboard template and keep it close at hand for reference.

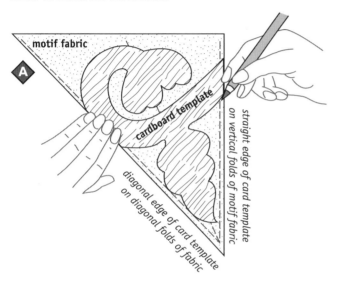

> **TIP** *Remember to add your seam allowance to all the edges of the motif at this stage, if you haven't already added it to your template.*

2 To cut out the motif, place the tacked, folded fabric on a flat surface; with a pair of sharp fabric scissors carefully cut along the marked pencil line (**B**), cutting through all the layers of fabric. After all the design has been cut out, remove any remaining tacking stitches and put the folded motif (**C**) to one side.

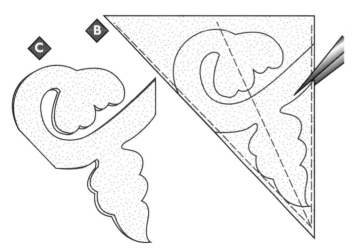

Positioning the motif

1 For this first stage, work with the folded background fabric only. Open up the folded fabric, place it right side up on a flat surface, and look for one quarter where the folds in the fabric have created three **grooves** (rather than **creases** – upwards folds) in the background fabric on the horizontal, diagonal and vertical lines. Turn the fabric around until that section is at the top left-hand side of the complete square (**A**).

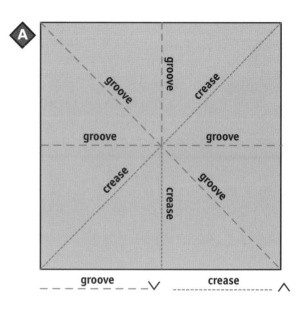

2 Next, place the unopened motif into the lower triangle of that quarter section, matching the diagonal and horizontal folds of the motif with the diagonal and horizontal grooves in the background fabric (**B**).

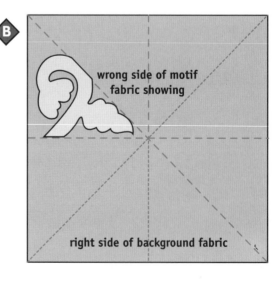

Open up the motif clockwise to a quarter fold, to marry with the vertical groove of the background fabric (**C**).

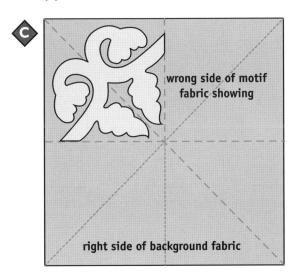

Continue opening the motif fabric clockwise onto the background fabric, matching the diagonal crease and the horizontal groove of the motif fabric to the diagonal crease and horizontal groove of the background fabric to reveal one half of the folded motif (**D**).

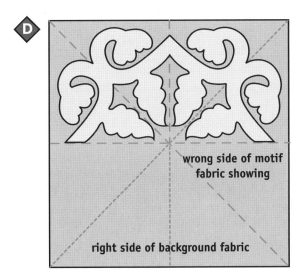

3 Finally, open the top layer of the folded motif fabric towards you; it will automatically fall into place with its folds matching the remaining grooves and creases of the background fabric. **Don't pull the motif to make it fit**; just gently pat it into position so that all its folds marry with the creases and grooves on the background fabric. The design is now centrally positioned on the background (**E**).

right side of motif fabric showing

4 It's essential to keep the fabric flat during the pinning and tacking stages; this will prevent any bunching of the background fabric under the motif.

> **TIP** *When you're pinning, you may find it helpful to work on the back of your cutting mat. Use the hard surface to your advantage; as the pin hits the board, try to tilt the pin upwards and back out through the motif surface. It takes a little practice but the end results are well worth it!*

It's much easier to use straight pins without glass-beaded heads; your sewing thread is less likely to get tangled around the large pinheads. Start pinning from the centre outwards on all of the vertical lines, then the horizontal lines, and finally the diagonal lines (**F**); in all cases make sure that you pin through both layers of fabric.

5 Next, pin around all of the cut edges of the motif (**G**). You'll need to use approximately fifty pins, if not more! The aim is to avoid any of the motif fabric from shifting while you're tacking the motif to the background surface.

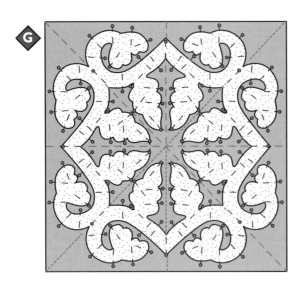

6 There are three reasons for tacking. First, it keeps the motif surface flat while you're appliquéing. Secondly, if you tack exactly ¼in (6mm) in from the raw edges it will give you the perfect ⅛in (3mm) turning. (There is an exception to this rule, which is explained on page 35.) Thirdly, during the needle turn appliqué, as the needle pushes the fabric back against the tacking line the fabric will lift and turn under automatically in one motion.

> **TIP** *On the diagrams, I've used a darker line to indicate the line of tacking stitches so that you can see it clearly, but I recommend that you use white or a light-coloured tacking thread; it will be easier to see when you're removing the tacking stitches after you've completed the appliqué.*

7 Work the lines of tacking in exactly the same order that you used for pinning the motif to the background fabric. Again try not to lift the fabric; it's essential that the appliqué surface remains flat so that both surfaces marry well when they're stitched together. With a large threaded tacking needle start from the centre point and work outwards on all the fold lines, stopping ½in (12mm) from the outside edge of the motif fabric on all the lines (**H**).

8 Then tack around the cut outside edges of the motif (**I**).

The general rule for a ⅛in (3mm) turning allowance is to tack ¼in (6mm) in from the cut edge – with one exception. When you reach each point, U or V, the turning allowance needs to be ½in (12mm) immediately on the point (**J**), around any deep,

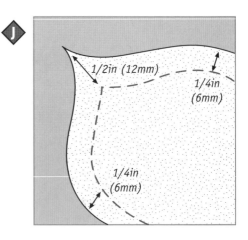

1/2in (12mm)

1/4in (6mm)

1/4in (6mm)

narrow curves (**K**), and to one side of each inward V. This will enable you to sculpt the fabric without having to cut through any tacking stitches. For inward Vs: if you're right-handed leave the ½in (12mm) gap on the right-hand side of the V each time as you tack (**L**); if you're left-handed, leave it on the left-hand side of each V (**M**). Once the tacking has been completed, remove all the pins.

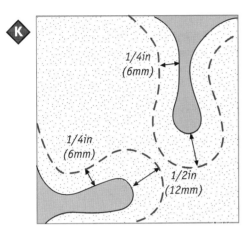

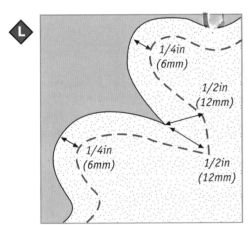

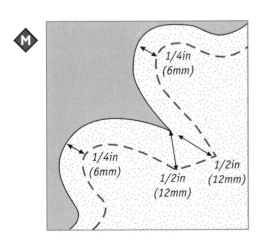

> **TIP** *If you find it difficult to estimate ¼in (6mm), keep an ordinary HB pencil beside you; you'll find that it measures ¼in (6mm) from edge to edge and can be used periodically to check that your measurements are accurate.*

Creating a one-quarter (1/4) design

To create a 1/4 design, you need to fold a square of fabric twice. The first two steps are exactly the same as steps 1 and 2 for the one-eighth fold, so you should be familiar with them by now! Just as before, it's essential to place the two squares of fabric side by side on the flat surface of your ironing board, right sides up, with the grains corresponding (**A**); this will enable you to fold both pieces of fabric in the same way at each stage.

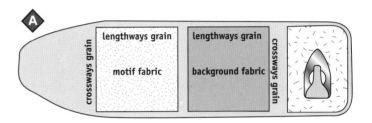

1 First, fold each of the two squares of fabric in half, right sides together, with the cut edges at the top; carefully press these first horizontal folds with a steam iron (**B**).

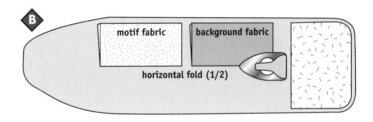

2 Next, fold each piece of fabric in half, right to left, matching corners, to create a quarter fold. Carefully press along the new vertical fold on each piece of fabric; start pressing from the outside cut edge and work in towards the centre point (**C**).

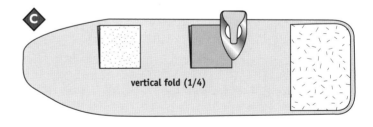

3 Unlike the technique for the one-eighth fold, for a one-quarter fold you'll need to tack around all four sides of the folded motif fabric square. With a large threaded tacking needle, stitch through all the layers of fabric along each side, starting ½in (12mm) in from the outside edge, then work two subsequent rows of tacking 1in (2.5cm) apart (**D**).

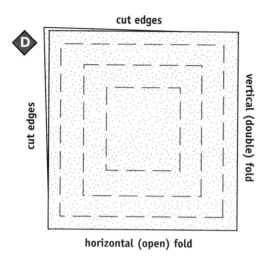

cut edges

cut edges

vertical (double) fold

horizontal (open) fold

Next, work a single row of tacking stitches diagonally from corner to corner, then repeating in the other direction to form a cross (**E**). Mark the motif design and cut it out in the usual way.

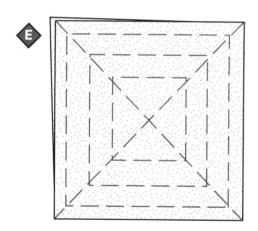

Unfolding a 1/4 design

Lay the open background fabric, right side up, on a flat surface (**A**). Lay the folded motif in the upper left quadrant, wrong side up, aligning the double fold of the motif fabric with the vertical groove in the background fabric and the open fold with the central horizontal groove (**B**).

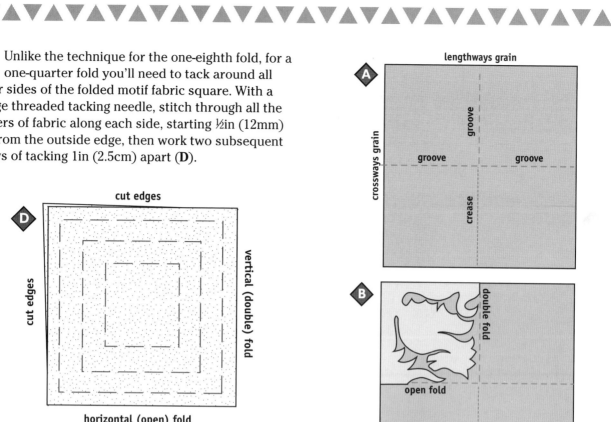

lengthways grain

crossways grain

groove

groove   groove

crease

double fold

open fold

Open the motif towards the upper right quadrant to a half fold, matching the central horizontal groove on the right-hand side (**C**), then unfold it towards you to reveal the right side of the motif fabric (**D**).

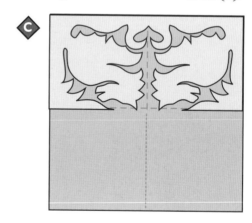

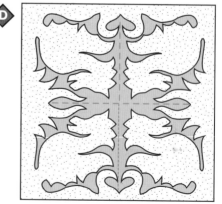

The single crease and all the grooves in the motif should align with the crease and grooves on the background fabric. **Do not pull the motif to fit**, otherwise it will distort; instead, gently pat the motif fabric in place. Then pin the motif to the background fabric. First pin along the vertical and horizontal folds, before pinning the inner motif edges and finally the straight cut outside edges. Follow the same order for tacking the two pieces together – you'll find extra guidelines for tacking on page 34.

Creating a one-sixth (1/6) design

For circular and square 1/6 designs, both the motif and the background fabric are folded in a completely different way from the one-eighth folds you're now familiar with.

Circular and hexagonal background settings

For circular and hexagonal designs, you must first fold both the motif and the background fabric in half diagonally; this enables you to mark the centre point of the folded line and then mark an accurate 60° angle on each side.

> **TIP** *As the squares of fabric are more difficult to fold on a narrow ironing board, I suggest that you make the first fold on a larger flat surface.*

1 Lay the motif and background fabric squares side by side on a flat surface, right sides up, with the grains corresponding. Fold the motif fabric in half diagonally (**A**), right sides together, making sure that the outside edges are level, to create a large triangle (**B**). Carefully transfer the motif fabric to your ironing board and press the first fold. As the diagonal fold lies along the bias, make sure that you don't stretch the fold while you're pressing it.

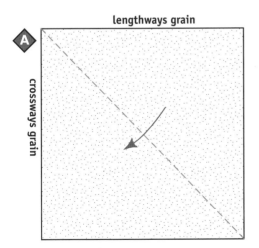

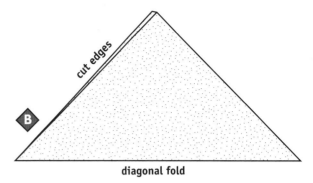

2 To divide the fabric into equal sections, you must first identify the centre point of the fold (and therefore of the square). To do this, fold the fabric in half again and press a small section where the diagonal fold meets the new vertical fold (**C**).

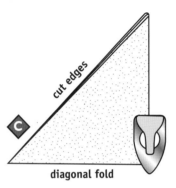

3 For the next step, you'll find it easier to return the fabric to a larger flat surface. Open the last fold to reveal the first diagonal fold and centre line (**D**). With a protractor measure a 60° angle each side of the centre fold (the 60° angles are measured from the diagonal fold), and mark the angles with an HB pencil. Then lay a ruler between the centre point and one marked angle and draw a faint pencil line; do the same with the angle on the other side (**E**).

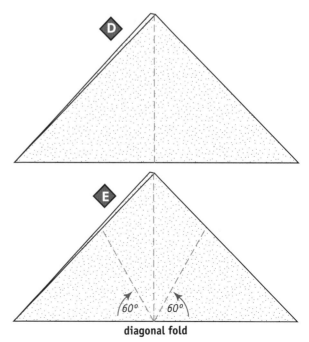

4 For the next step, it's essential to make sure that the two 60° folds are perfectly aligned, so that your motif will be accurate. First, fold the fabric from left to right along the marked line, so that the creased edge rests exactly against the angled line you've marked to the right of the centre point (**F**). (I find that it helps to place a ruler along the marked line; by folding the fabric over the ruler, you then end up with the fold in just the right position.) Then fold the right-hand side of the fabric across, on the marked line, so that the creased edge exactly aligns with the 60° line to the left of the centre point (**G**).

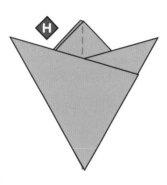

5 Before pressing the new folds, check that the folded fabric underneath is lying flat against the 60° line, and hasn't become crumpled or moved its position. Carefully lift the folded fabric to your ironing board and press the two new folds.

6 Repeat the entire procedure for the background fabric (**H**). You now have two shapes, folded in exactly the same way.

7 Transfer your design onto the tacked motif fabric (**I**), and cut out the motif in the usual way (**J**).

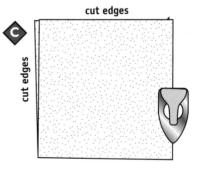

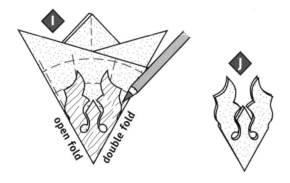

TIP *It's much easier to mark and cut a circular or hexagonal edge on the background fabric while it's still folded.*

Square background settings

1 Lay the two squares of fabric (one square of background fabric, one of motif fabric) side by side on a flat surface, right sides up and grains aligning. Fold the square of motif fabric in half vertically or horizontally (**A**).

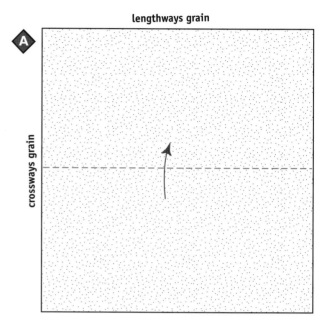

2 Fold this rectangle in half again (**B**) and press to mark the centre line (**C**).

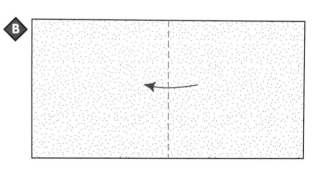

3 Open the last fold to reveal the first vertical or horizontal fold line and centre point. With a protractor measure a 60° angle either side of the centre line and mark these angles with an HB pencil (**D**). Remember that each 60° angle is measured from the folded edge of the fabric.

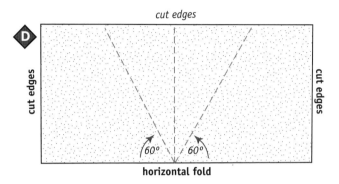

4 Fold the left section over to meet the 60° angle to the right of the centre point (**E**), and then the right section over to meet the 60° angle to the left of the centre point (**F**).

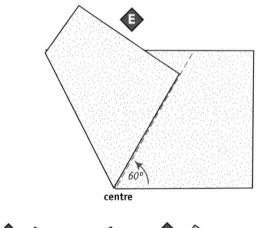

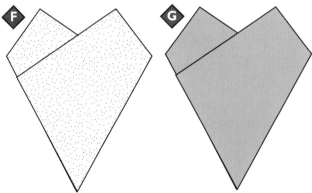

5 Fold the square of background fabric in exactly the same way (**G**). Transfer your design onto the tacked motif fabric (**H**), and cut out the motif in the usual way (**I**). (For details of the best way to tack a 1/6 design, see page 73.)

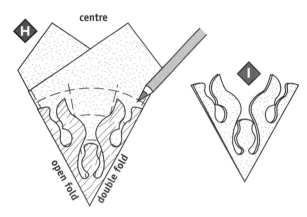

An alternative way to fold the fabric for a square background setting is as follows. Fold the fabric in half diagonally. To divide the square into equal sections, fold the triangle in half again to mark the centre line. Open the last fold to reveal the first diagonal fold and centre point, then follow steps 4 and 5 as described above.

Unfolding a 1/6 design

1 Unfold the background fabric right side up on a flat surface (**A**). If your first fold was horizontal, lay the motif design, wrong side up, into the middle third division of the background fabric with the open fold to the left diagonal line (**B**).

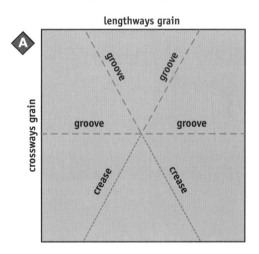

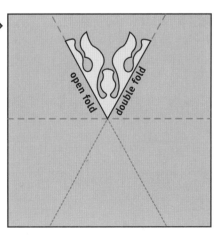

2 Open the first folded section from left to right (**C**); then open the second fold from right to left (**D**). At this point each fold should be in alignment with the four grooves on the top half of the background fabric.

If the first fold in your background fabric was vertical follow the sequence shown in **F**. If your first fold was diagonal, follow the sequence shown in **G**. For unfolding circular and hexagonal settings, follow the sequence shown in **H** 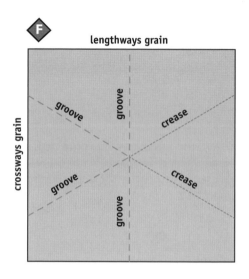on page 42.

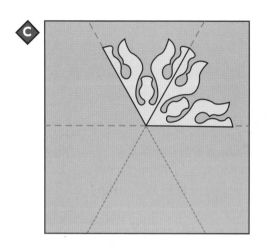

Sequence F

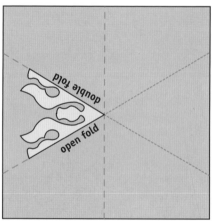

3 Open the final fold towards you, matching the two creases in the bottom half (**E**); only now will you see the correct side of the motif fabric. **Do not pull the motif to fit**, otherwise it will distort: instead, gently pat the motif fabric in place. Continue with the pinning and tacking as for a 1/8 design.

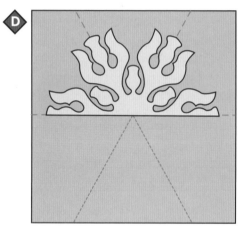

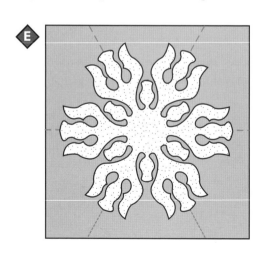

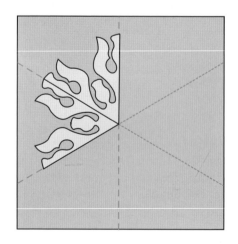

RIGHT-HANDED

LEFT-HANDED

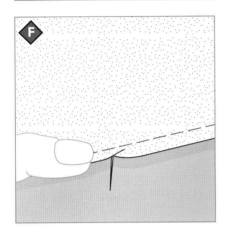

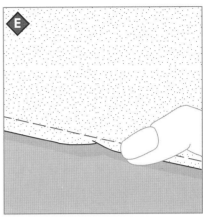

2 Before you begin any stitching, flick the needle to the right. This will turn under a small amount of the motif edge to form the first fold; use your thumbnail to crease the new fold (**E**).

3 To make your first stitch, insert the threaded needle at an angle from the back of your work and bring it out through the creased fold. This will anchor and hide the knot under the motif's edge (**F**).

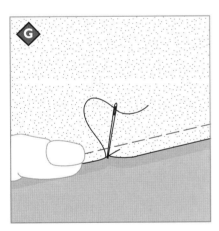

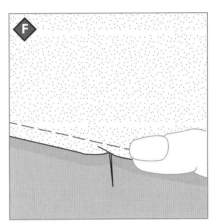

4 Now insert the needle straight down into the background fabric, immediately in front of the thread in the creased fold. The needle will brush against the folded edge before entering the background fabric again (**G**). Only after the needle has begun to enter the background fabric can you start tilting it to the left; move it forward on the underneath surface for approximately ¹⁄₁₆in (1.5mm) and then tilt it upwards to exit on the creased fold once again (**H**). Continue working in the same way until the whole motif has been appliquéd to the background fabric.

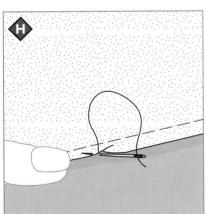

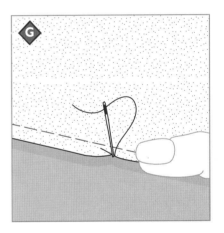

> **TIPS** *Never place the needle in front or behind the thread where it exits the creased edge, as this will ultimately lead to visible stitches on the motif surface. If the stitches are too loose or not close enough together, the motif edge will open up and in certain cases reveal loose threads or small sections of the cut edge. Don't pull the stitches too tight, as this will cause small indentations and puckering on the motif edge.*

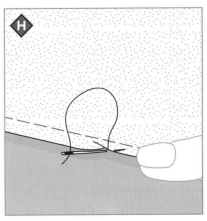

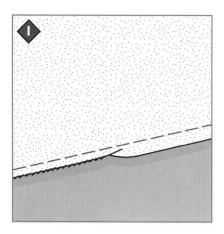

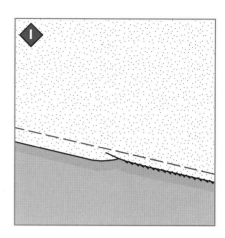

5 It's impossible to turn under large sections of the motif edge in one go, so work only ½in (12mm) ahead of the stitched line at a time. This will also help you to maintain a smooth straight or curved line. Continue to work the stitches roughly ⅟₁₆in (1.5-2mm) apart so that you get approximately 12-14 stitches to the inch (2.5cm), and try to maintain the same tension for each stitch (**I**). The aim is for the motif edge to nestle flat against the surface of the background fabric.

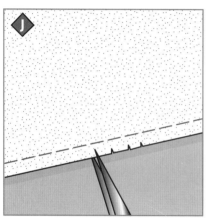

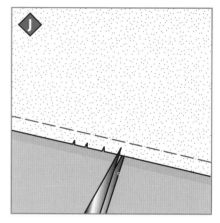

6 There's no need to clip all the curves as most of the cut edges of a one-eighth pattern are on the bias. Occasionally you will need to clip – for example, when part of the design is on the straight of the grain and your needle meets resistance: the fabric will curl instead of folding back smoothly. When clipping is necessary, remember to make only small clips, approximately ⅟₁₆in (1.5mm) in from the outside edge of the fabric (**J**). This will enable you to sculpt the fabric edge without meeting any further resistance or losing the shape of the motif outline (**K**).

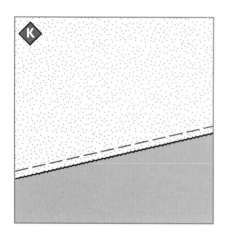

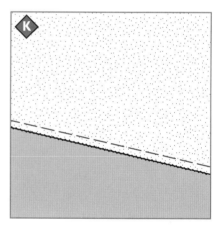

Frequently the end of the thread begins to fray because of the constant friction as you pull it against the eye of the needle as you appliqué. There's no way you can prevent this from happening, but at the same time you don't want to appliqué with a split thread. Work until the last 3-4 inches of thread, then take the needle through to the back of your work; make two back-stitches on top of each other inside the sewing line, then run the needle about an inch (2.5cm) between the two layers to hide the thread. Bring the (still threaded) needle out back onto the surface, then gently pull the thread before trimming the loose end close to the surface; the trimmed end will then automatically spring back and remain hidden between the layers of fabric.

Making perfect points

This new method for working perfect points (and also narrow, deep concave curves and inward Vs) will give you astonishing results which you can, in future, apply to any appliqué technique! Whether you're working on a short or elongated point the principle remains the same. This technique will produce a smooth, flat, perfect point, time after time without too much effort.

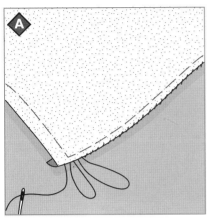

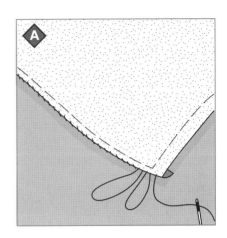

1 Sew up to the last three stitches away from a point. Make the next two stitches into independent loops (loops are ordinary stitches which haven't been closed out, or pulled through); the place where the sewing thread then exits the fold is where the point will eventually be located (**A**). For elongated points only, cut off the triangle that protrudes, so that the fabric is flush with the motif edge (**B**).

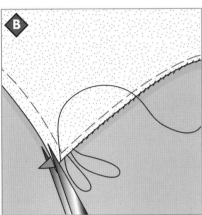

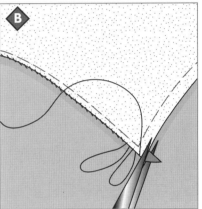

> **TIP** *Make one loop larger than the other; this will stop the two loops from crossing, which would prevent you from pulling them closed.*

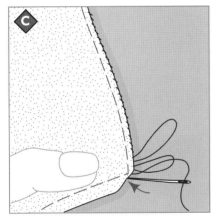

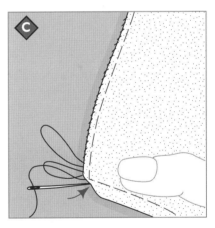

2 Turn the fabric around anticlockwise so that the cut edge of the new sewing line is facing you. Place your thumb behind the tacking (basting) line on the new row while turning under the point. With the tip of the appliqué needle, fold the top of the point back under for approximately ½in (12mm) as shown in **C**, and also fold under a small section of the turning allowance at the beginning of the motif edge on the opposite side (**D**).

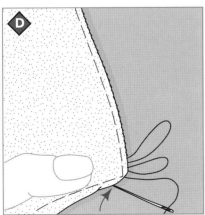

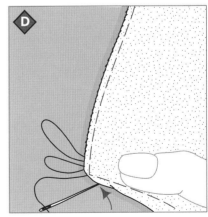

RIGHT-HANDED

LEFT-HANDED

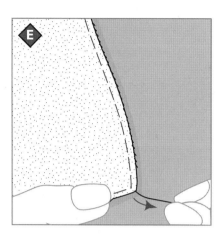

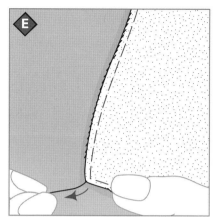

3 Hold the turned area securely between finger and thumb while gently pulling the thread. This action pulls through the two looped stitches, and automatically brings the tip out to the right position, while the new seam stays tucked under (**E**). Continue sewing along the new edge (**F**).

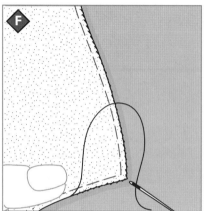

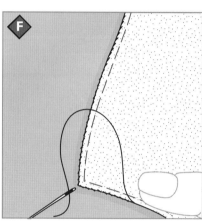

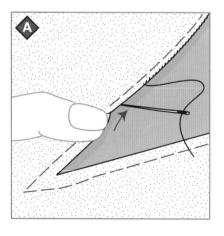

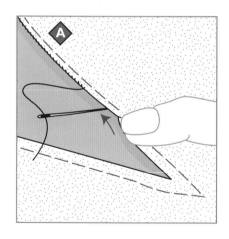

RIGHT-HANDED

Inward Vs

LEFT-HANDED

These are worked differently from the rest of the appliqué. Work as normal (**A**) until you're ½in (12mm) from the V; at this point the turning allowance will begin to narrow. To achieve a perfect inward V, you'll need to change the direction in which you sweep the turned fabric under on each side. Often when people appliqué, the turning allowance on the opposite side is sculpted away from the V; this causes distortion in the fabric, and in some cases results in frayed edges that are difficult to remedy. To prevent any distortion or fraying it's vital that, on each side, you always work into the V with the needle.

▼▲▼▲▼▲▼▲▼▲▼▲▼▲▼▲▼▲▼▲▼▲▼▲▼▲▼

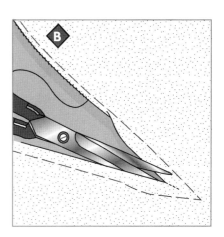

1 Turn the appliqué around, so that the centre of the V is towards you. You may find it helpful to draw a faint line on the fabric surface in the centre of the V or make an indentation mark with your thumbnail, before sculpting under the first side of the turning allowance. For deep inward Vs, clip the turning allowance in the centre of the V just over ⅟₁₆in (1.5mm) in from the outside edge (**B**).

2 Using the needle tip, sculpt the fabric under into the middle of the marked V with a clean sweeping action; at the same time, push the opposite side back almost to a right angle (**C** and **D**). To achieve this, you may need to take one or two clean sweeping movements of the needle.

3 Hold the creased edge firmly between your thumb and forefinger, then stitch into the middle of the V (**E**).

> **TIP** *To avoid disturbing the cut edges in the deep inward Vs unnecessarily, it's advisable to work a stab stitch in the centre of the V. I find that it helps to insert your needle at an angle under the turned motif's edge, and not vertically into the background fabric. Then, from underneath your work, angle the needle to come back out through the turned edge.*

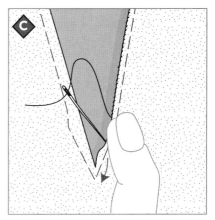

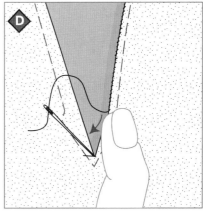

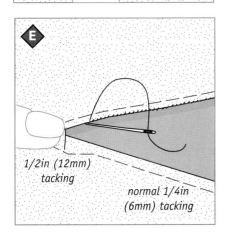

1/2in (12mm) tacking

normal 1/4in (6mm) tacking

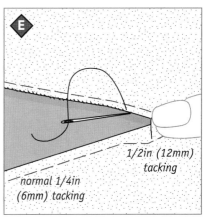

1/2in (12mm) tacking

normal 1/4in (6mm) tacking

RIGHT-HANDED

LEFT-HANDED

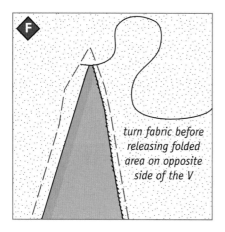

turn fabric before releasing folded area on opposite side of the V

4 Turn the fabric round so that you're now looking into the V (**F**). Next, release the folded fabric at right angles. Place the tip of your needle onto the fabric surface, sculpting the seam allowance in towards the V with the needle tip (**G**); then continue to stitch away from the V as normal along the new turned edge.

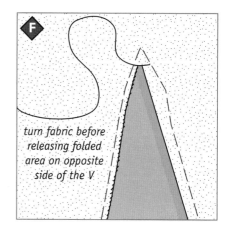

turn fabric before releasing folded area on opposite side of the V

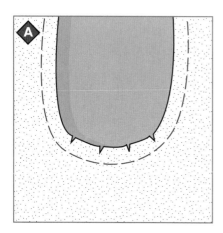

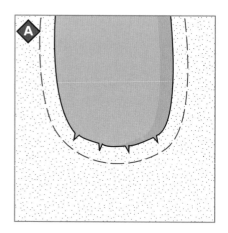

RIGHT-HANDED

Curves

LEFT-HANDED

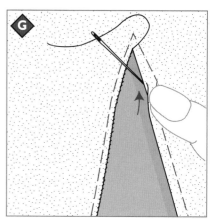

For concave (inward) curves, if you're working with a ⅛in (3mm) turning allowance there's rarely any need to clip the edges, as most of the curves will lie on the bias of the fabric. For turning allowances larger than ⅛in (3mm), you will need to clip the edges to enable you to distribute the turned fabric evenly. You only need to clip the fabric edge when your needle meets resistance and the turned edge starts to curl instead of folding under flat. This will vary depending on the severity of the inward curve, and indicates that the fabric edge is on the straight of the grain; you will need to clip only that section of the design (**A**). The curve on the crossways grain will require fewer clips compared with the curve on the lengthways (selvedge) grain, as the former has much more give.

Right-Handed   *Left-Handed*

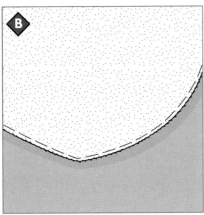

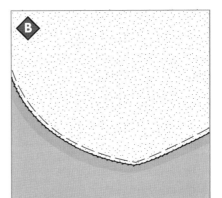

For convex (outward) curves there is more material to distribute evenly when the edge is turned under; therefore you don't need to clip the outside edges for the turned fabric to lie flat. Equally, it's impossible to turn under large sections of the seam allowance at one time; if you try to do this, peaks can appear on the sewn edge (**B**). To prevent this from happening, it's better to work the curve in small sections. Turn under ⅛in (3mm) seam allowance, ease the tucked fabric where necessary, then hold the turned seam allowance securely between your thumb and finger while sewing the motif edge to the background fabric with one or two close stitches (**C**). As you near the top of the curve there will be more tucked fabric to distribute evenly. I find it helps to place the tip of the needle on the underneath surface of the tucked fabric while gently easing the turned fabric back towards the stitched line so that it lies flat (**D**). This prevents any distortion on the turned motif edge (**E**).

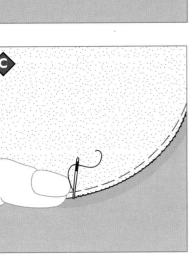

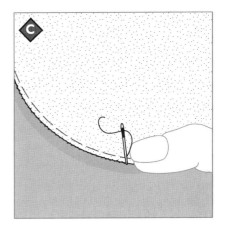

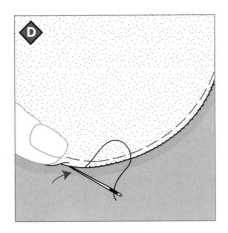

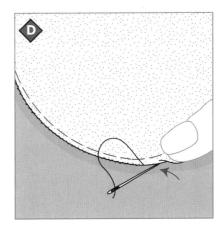

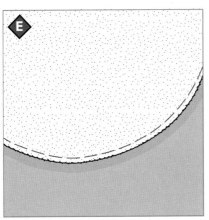

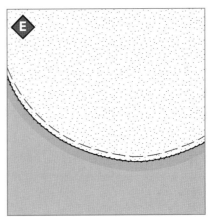

Embellishing and quilting

When all of the appliqué is completed – and not before! – all the tacking stitches can be removed. Next, place the design wrong side up on a padded ironing board and press it carefully with a steam iron, to remove all of the creases and fold lines before you assemble the block.

Wawae moa (chicken feet stitch)

Today some quilters still use this stitch, usually as an embellishment after the motif has been appliquéd to the background fabric. It's a simple yet effective type of embroidery, worked over the turned, pressed motif edge before you prepare the appliqué top for quilting.

The stitch is worked in three stages, with one shorter stitch set at an angle at each side of the longer straight central stitch.

1 Bring the needle up at point **a**, then insert it again at point **b**, over the motif edge and into the background fabric. Pull the thread through (**A**).

2 Next, bring the needle up at point **c** and insert it straight downwards into point **b**, once again pulling the thread through (**B**).

3 For the final step, bring the needle out at point **d**; insert the needle at an angle back down into point **b**, pulling the thread through to complete the sequence (**C**).

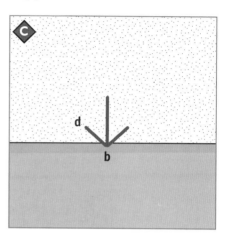

4 Continue working the composite stitches in the same way at equal intervals around the edge of the motif (**D**). I work each stitch the same length until I approach a point; I then gradually shorten the stitch length as I work around the point, then gradually lengthen it again to the normal size (**E**).

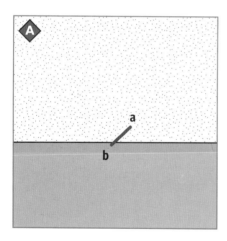

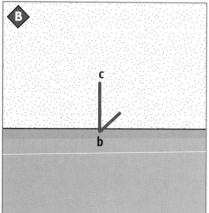

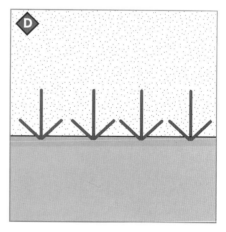

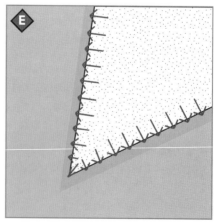

Quilting

1 Always cut the backing fabric and wadding 2in (5cm) larger than the appliqué quilt top; mistakes can happen during tacking and quilting, so allow a little extra on all sides. Before sandwiching the block together, make sure that all loose threads have been removed from the reverse side of the appliqué block, no appliqué threads are protruding from the motif edge, and any loose threads have been removed from the cut wadding. Although it's not impossible to remove the threads once the block has been sandwiched, it is more awkward – and certainly time-consuming.

TIP *Open the wadding out flat at least 24 hours before use to remove any creases and fold lines.*

2 Next, put the layers of the block together. Start with the pressed backing fabric, wrong side up, on a flat surface; cover this with the wadding, and finally the appliquéd block right side up (**A**). What you do next will depend on whether you'll be quilting with or without a frame. Whether to use a frame or not is a very personal decision, and we all have our own favourite method; I don't actually tack (baste) my sandwiched block together, as I put it straight onto a plastic quilting frame which eliminates the need for tacking. If you don't use a frame, or use a less rigid quilting frame than mine, secure the layers together with a grid of horizontal and vertical lines of tacking at regular intervals.

3 There are three basic steps to quilting a Hawaiian appliqué block, and they're usually worked in the following order:

• Outline the entire motif on the background fabric as close to the motif edge as possible (**B**). This is similar to quilting in the ditch.

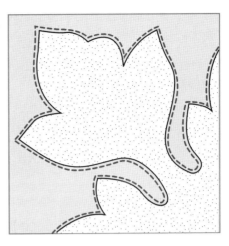

• Traditionally you then echo the motif shape inside the appliquéd design – or you may decide to choose a more contemporary style by emphasising the patterns of fruit shapes, flower petals or veins of the leaf. Whichever style you decide on, the first row of quilting stitches on the motif should begin ½in (12mm) in from the folded edge. If you're using the traditional method, work separate, evenly-spaced rows of quilting towards the centre of the motif (**C**). If you're going for a contemporary look, work lines where you think they look most effective (**D**).

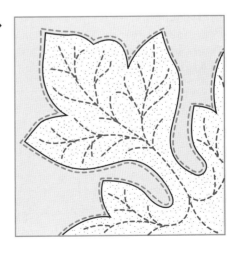

• Finally, follow the outline of the motif shape on the background fabric, working separate rows of stitching ½-1in (1.2-2.5cm) apart radiating out from the central motif. This is representative of the waves around the islands' shores (**E**).

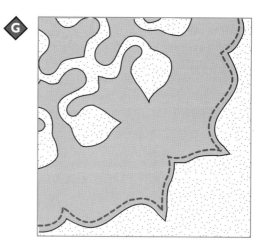

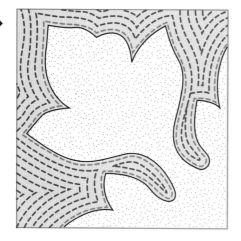

Blending

If you want to use echo quilting on a design with a central motif and a border (**F**), use the technique known as blending.

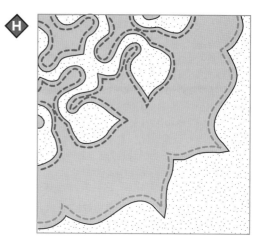

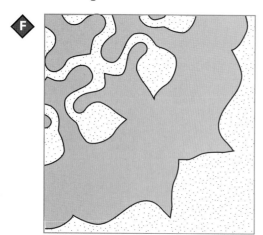

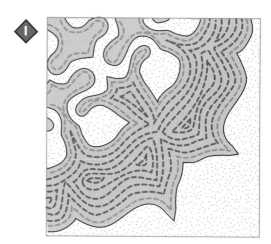

For blending, the rows are worked alternately round the border (**G**) and then round the motif (**H**), carrying on alternating until they meet (**I**). This technique creates a more harmonious sequence of quilting lines than if you worked out from the centre until the echo lines bumped into the border.

PROJECTS

Now you're familiar with the basic techniques of designing patterns, making templates, and folding, marking, cutting out and appliquéing the motifs, it's time to try one of the projects. In this section of the book there are fourteen projects; I recommend that you start with *New Beginnings*. This is designed specifically for you to practise the art of needle turn appliqué and perfect points without having to worry – just yet! – about those awkward deep inward Vs.

All the templates for the projects have a ⅛in (3mm) seam allowance included in them. Most of the templates are full size, and just need to be photocopied or traced; a few will need to be enlarged on a photocopier by the percentage mentioned next to the template.

All the fabrics specified in the materials lists are 44/45in (112/114cm) wide unless I've mentioned otherwise. When ⅝yd (0.5m) of fabric is specified for the various 18in (46cm) cushions, make sure that you have a generous half metre – half a yard won't give you a large-enough square for the motif and background fabric. I've given measurements in both imperial and metric, but when you're stitching, use only one system throughout.

To avoid lots of repetition of the basic techniques and tips, you'll find that the instructions for the different projects cross-refer to the techniques section. If you need extra reminders, check back to the relevant pages; as you grow more confident, you'll find that you need to cross-refer less and less.

THE PROJECTS

1
2
3

4
5
6

7
8
9
10

11
12
13
14

New Beginnings (Ascot 2000)

Finished size:
18in (46cm) square

This abstract pattern was taken from a series of trial paper cuts produced for a college portfolio. It wasn't until much later I saw the potential of this simple shape as a perfect project to practise my new techniques for needle turn appliqué and perfect points. For the motif I've chosen to use a printed fabric instead of two contrasting colours, and you'll see from the photograph below that I've used both the positive and negative shapes to make two appliquéd cushion (pillow) covers. As this is the first project in the book, I'll explain all the stages in great detail; all the other cushion cover designs I've included (see pages 61-71) are produced in the same way. The full-size template for this design is on page 95.

New Beginnings; positive shape (left) and negative shape (right); contemporary colourway, hand appliqué with traditional contour quilting

MATERIALS

▲ motif fabric: ⅝yd (0.5m) patterned or solid-coloured cotton fabric; this measurement includes enough fabric for the bias binding

▲ background fabric: 1½yd (1.4m) calico (muslin); this measurement includes enough fabric for the cushion lining and backing sections of the cushion cover

▲ wadding (batting): 21in (54cm) square of Hobbs Thermore or 2oz polyester wadding

▲ 2½yd (2.3m) white piping cord

OTHER REQUIREMENTS

▲ basic sewing kit

▲ appliqué and quilting needles

▲ white tacking (basting) thread

▲ sewing thread to match your motif fabric

▲ quilting thread

▲ thin card (eg a cereal box), sharp paper scissors and permanent marker

▲ HB propelling (automatic) pencil and ball-point pen

▲ quilters' clear plastic ruler, 24 x 6in

▲ rotary cutter and cutting mat

▲ masking tape

▲ 18in (46cm) cushion (pillow) pad

Making the template

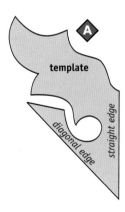

1 Photocopy (or trace carefully) the motif design on page 95. Lay the photocopy face down on a flat surface and, with a soft pencil, rub over the outline of the shape on the back of the paper.

2 Lay the card on a flat surface and secure it with masking tape. Position the drawing right side up on top and, with a ball-point pen, draw round the outline of the motif. Check that the outlines of the design are visible on the surface of the card; if not, go over the outline again. Once the lines have been transferred, remove the paper.

3 Use the paper scissors to cut out the cardboard template. With a permanent marker label the centre, diagonal and straight lines on the appropriate outside edges of the template (**A**).

TIP *If you prefer, you can simply cut out the photocopy, stick it onto the card, and cut round it, rather than using the method above.*

Cutting the fabric

4 From the motif fabric, cut one 19½in (49.5cm) square for the appliqué motif and one 18in (46cm) square for the quick strip bias binding. From the background fabric, first cut one 19½in (49.5cm) square for the appliqué background, and one 21in (53.5cm) square

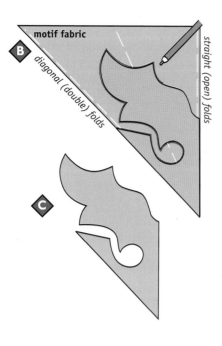

for the lining. Then cut one 19 x 10½in (48.5 x 27cm) rectangle and one 19 x 14½in (48.5 x 37cm) rectangle; these will be used to make the envelope closure for the cushion cover.

Preparing the motif

5 Fold both the motif and the background fabric squares into right-angled triangles and secure the motif fabric shape with tacking (basting) stitches. (See pages 30-31 for comprehensive instructions and diagrams for folding, pressing and tacking.)

6 Place the 1/8 cardboard template onto the folded and tacked motif fabric, aligning the diagonal and straight edges; using a fabric marking pencil, trace round the motif outline onto the motif fabric (**B**). (See page 32 for full instructions and diagrams for marking.)

7 With a sharp pair of fabric scissors, carefully cut out the folded motif along the marked lines (**C**); remember to leave the connectors on the diagonal and straight fold intact so that you end up with the correct repeat pattern when the fabric is unfolded. (See page 32 for hints on cutting out the motif.)

8 Lay the background fabric square on a flat surface and open it up so that the right side of the fabric is facing you. Lay the folded motif on top, wrong side up, and follow the instructions on pages 32-33 to open it up in the correct order and align the folds and creases (**D-F**); as you unfold the final fold towards you, the right side of the fabric will be revealed (**G**).

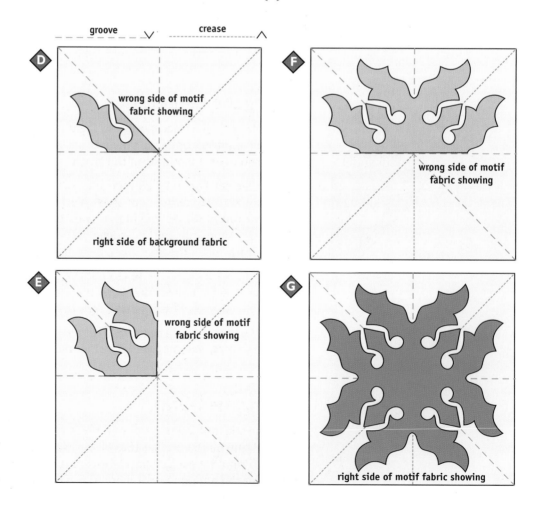

9 Pin the motif in place, beginning at the centre and working outwards along all the fold lines, then pinning the outside cut edges. (Check back to pages 33-34 for detailed instructions on pinning.) Follow the instructions on page 34 to tack the motif fabric to the background fabric.

Needle turn appliqué

10 Thread an appliqué needle with about 20in (50cm) of thread to match your motif fabric. Appliqué the turned motif edge to the background fabric, following the detailed instructions on pages 44-48 for the basic technique and the points.

Quilting

11 Once all the appliqué has been completed, remove the tacking stitches. Place the design face down on a padded ironing surface and press on the reverse side only.

12 Lay the pressed lining for the cushion cover front right side down on a flat surface; cover this with the wadding, aligning the cut edges of the wadding with the raw edges of the fabric square. Then position the pressed appliqué design on top, right side up, on top of the wadding (**H**). Whether or not you tack the layers together will depend on the method you're using for quilting.

13 Now it's time to quilt your cushion cover. The way you quilt will be very much a personal choice, and will also depend on the fabric you're using; only you can decide how much quilting is right for a particular project.On page 53 I explain the three different stages of quilting a traditional Hawaiian appliqué design; you may want to adapt or omit one or more of these stages.

New Beginnings (positive shape); detail showing hand appliqué with traditional contour quilting

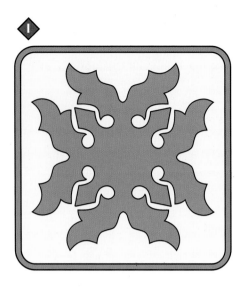

Finishing

14 Using the clear plastic ruler trim away the excess wadding and lining to leave an accurate 19in (48.5cm) square. Follow the instructions on page 90 for quick-strip bias binding, cutting the strips 1½in (4cm) wide; you'll need a total of 2½yd (2.3m) of binding. Use this strip to cover the piping cord (see page 91), then add this to the front of the cushion cover (**I**); follow the details on page 94 to make an envelope closure for the cushion cover.

I've also used the negative (border) shape – basically the cut-off from the folded motif fabric – to create a second cushion cover design. If you refer back to page 29, diagram D shows you how to re-shape the diagonal fold to eliminate the small extra V. To make a second cushion you'll need the same fabric requirements as listed before, but this time you'll only need a fat quarter of motif fabric (for the bias binding) – the motif is the negative shape (offcut) from the previous design. To position the border motif, fold the 19½in (49.5cm) square of background fabric into a right-angled triangle, then open it up, right side up, on a flat surface. Place the folded motif on the top left triangle as before, aligning the straight cut edges of the folded motif and the background fabric, and aligning the diagonal and horizontal grooves (**A**). Unfold the motif in the usual way until the right side of the complete motif is revealed (**B-D**), then appliqué the inside edge of the motif, quilt the design and make up the cushion cover as before; the only difference is that this time you're creating a border design, which gives you the chance to place more emphasis on the contour quilting in the negative space.

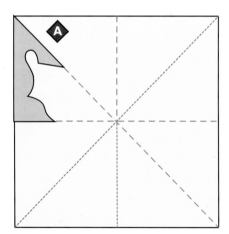

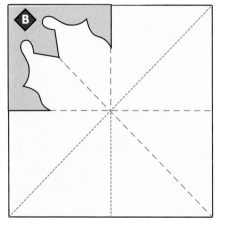

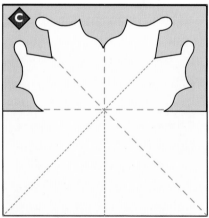

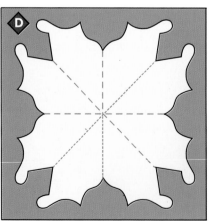

New Beginnings (negative shape); detail showing hand appliqué with traditional contour quilting

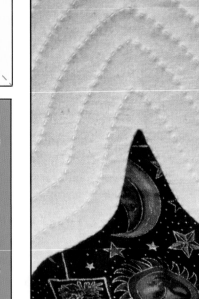

The following six cushion cover projects are all the same size as **New Beginnings**, *(apart from Glorious William, which is a little larger), and are all produced using exactly the same methods. The requirements are also the same as those listed on page 57 – just alter the colours of the motif and background fabrics as necessary. Once the appliqué of each design is finished, you can quilt it as you wish, and to suit the fabrics you've chosen.*

Michael's Choice

Finished size:
18in (46cm) square

My son selected the colour-scheme for this cushion – hence the name! The inspiration for the simple motif design was taken from a carved wooden banister at Bentley Priory. For the motif I used a maroon-coloured designer fabric, and appliquéd it onto solid black; this creates a totally different impression from stitching a coloured motif onto a white or cream background. The full-size template for this design is on page 96.

Michael's Choice (right, and detail below); contemporary colourway, hand appliqué with traditional contour quilting

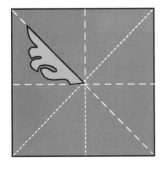
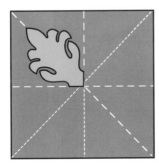
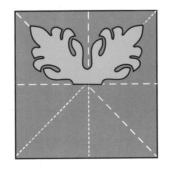
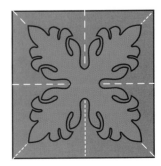

Mighty Oak

Finished size:
18in (46cm) square

I've chosen the acorn as the emblem of England because this will always evoke wonderful memories of our walks in Windsor Great Park with Beth, our crazy border collie. We had such enormous fun, playing hide-and-seek behind the old majestic oak trees, much to Beth's consternation!

For this design, I've made two cushion covers so that, when they're placed side by side, you can see at a glance the contrast between using a traditional and a contemporary colour-scheme. The traditional use of two solid colours, red and white, creates a bold, striking contrast between the motif and background fabric. The contemporary colour-way, which uses a designer motif fabric and a soft mottled cream background, is much more subdued, with less differentiation between the two fabrics. Both the cushion front panels were quilted using a contemporary design, but you can see that the stitching is less obvious on the surface of the designer fabric. The full-size template for this design is on page 97.

Mighty Oak; contemporary colourway, hand appliqué with traditional and contemporary contour quilting

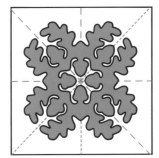

Mighty Oak (right, and detail below right); traditional colourway, hand appliqué with traditional and contemporary contour quilting

Detail of the contemporary colourway (below), showing hand appliqué with traditional and contemporary contour quilting

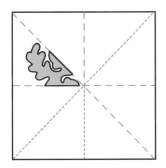

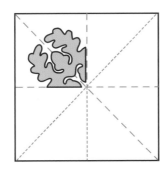

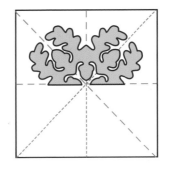

Heart of Ivy

Finished size:
18in (46cm) square

One of my students, Audrey d'Oliveira, bought the batik fabric on this cushion cover, simply because she was drawn to the rich warm colours, but having no particular project in mind. At a one-day workshop with me, she decided that the moment had come to use the fabric. Using three ivy leaves for inspiration, I drew a simple motif shape – which coincidentally complements the patterns on the batik fabric. Audrey appliquéd and quilted the design; it was made with love for her dearest and oldest friend, in her favourite colours, as a gift for Christmas. The full-size template for this design is on page 98.

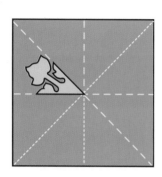

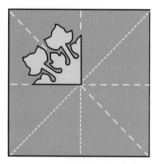

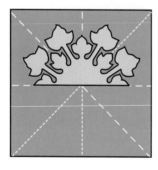

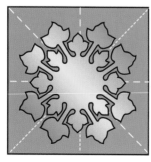

Heart of Ivy (above, and detail below); contemporary colourway, hand appliqué with traditional contour quilting

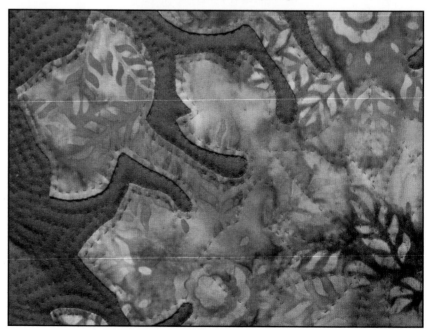

Mountain Glory

Finished size:
18in (46cm) square

A plant called *Blasippan*, which primarily grows in Scandinavia, provided the inspiration for the design elements for this cushion cover (pillow cover). I used both the young and the mature three-lobed leaf shapes to create the 1/8 pattern which I've called *Mountain Glory*. I like to use the bright Amish colourways for my Hawaiian appliqué, and I've recently begun experimenting with using a Hoffman printed fabric instead of a solid-coloured fabric for the motif; I've done the same in this project, but you can use any fabric you like the look of. As the fabric already had a strong design element, I omitted step 2 of the traditional quilting (see page 53). The full-size template for this design is on page 99.

Mountain Glory (right, and detail below); contemporary colourway, hand appliqué with traditional contour quilting

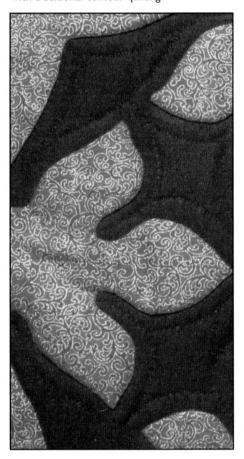

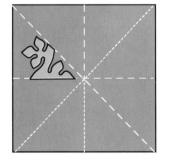
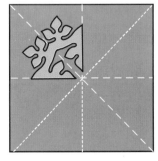
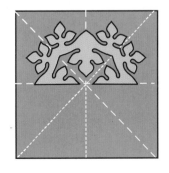

Christmas Rose

Finished size:
18in (46cm) square

Looking out of the conservatory window for divine inspiration, my gaze was immediately drawn to my favourite winter flower, the Christmas rose. Part of the design element was drawn to reflect the graceful nodding flowers. Rather than use a seasonal colour-scheme for the motif, I chose my two favourite colours instead; the motif fabric is a purple cotton batik, and the background is a solid lilac cotton. The full-size template for this design is on page 100.

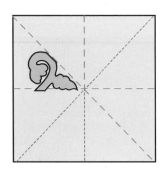

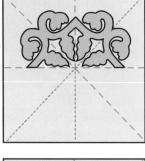

Christmas Rose (above, and detail below); contemporary colourway, hand appliqu;
with traditional contour quilting

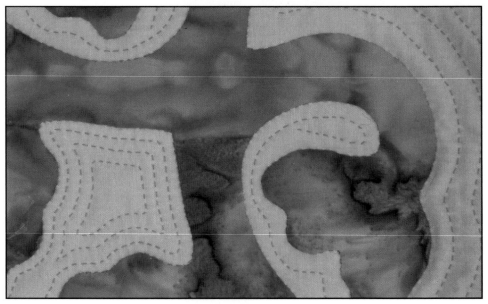

Irish Fortune

Finished size:
18in (46cm) square

The design elements here reflect the close friendship with our dearest and oldest American friends Charlie and Nora, and Nora's late parents Bridie and Tom who emigrated from Ireland to the United States. Also, I was born on the 17th March, St Patrick's Day! The four hearts represent cherished memories of our stay in the United States when my husband worked in Washington DC, and our subsequent and frequent holidays with Charlie and Nora. The motif fabric is a green cotton batik, appliquéd onto white calico (muslin). The full-size template for this design is on page 101.

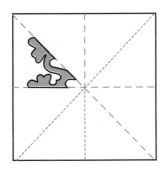

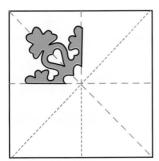

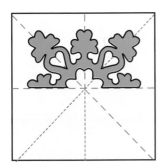

Irish Fortune (above, and detail below); contemporary colourway, hand appliqué with traditional and contemporary contour quilting

Highland Guardian

Finished size:
18in (46cm) square

I've always been drawn towards the Art Nouveau period for its elegant flowing and meandering designs. This pattern features the 'whiplash' line which characterised the Art Nouveau period, and a stylised version of the thistle, the Scottish emblem. According to legend, the Guardian Thistle was so named because it evoked an anguished cry from a marauding Viking who trod upon it, and so alerted the sleeping Scottish defenders. The design incorporates a barb or prickle in each corner. The full-size template for this design is on page 102.

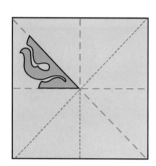

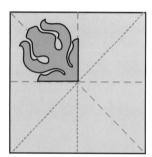

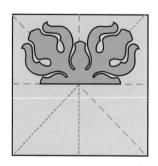

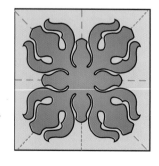

Highland Guardian (above, and detail below); traditional colourway, hand appliqué with traditional and contemporary contour quilting

Glorious William

Finished size: 20in (51cm) square
(traditional setting),
or 22in (56cm) square
(on point setting)

The same stylised motif and fabric colours have been used here to demonstrate how two different layouts for a 1/8 fold will alter the appearance of the finished design. Placing the longest side of the template on the diagonal fold (traditional layout – see page 18) forms a square design (a), whereas placing the longest side of the template on the straight fold (that is, on point – see page 18) results in a cross-shaped motif (b). This design is a little larger than the others in this section; when the traditional 1/8 placement is used the motif fits on a 20in (51cm) square, and when it's set on point it fits on a 22in (56cm) square background. The method of producing, appliquéing, quilting and finishing the cover is the same as for *New Beginnings* (see pages 56-60). The full-size template for this design is on page 103.

a   b

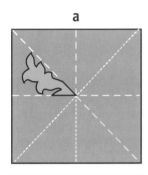
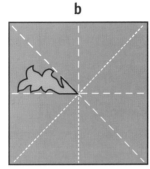
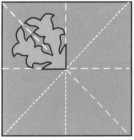
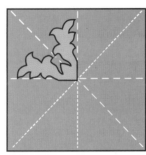
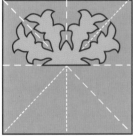
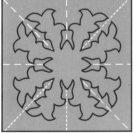

Glorious William; traditional layout (top) and
on point layout (below); contemporary colourway,
hand appliqué with traditional contour quilting

MATERIALS

Traditional 1/8 fold placement
Finished size:
20in (51cm) square

▲ motif fabric: 20in (51cm) square patterned or solid-coloured cotton fabric

▲ background and backing fabric: 22in (56cm) square solid black cotton fabric, plus one 21 x 13in (53.5 x 33cm) and one 21 x 17in (53.5 x 43cm) rectangle

▲ lining fabric: 24in (61cm) square of calico (muslin)

▲ wadding (batting): 24in (61cm) square of Hobbs Thermore or 2oz polyester wadding

▲ 2¾yd (2.6m) white piping cord

▲ 2¾yd (2.6m) bias binding

▲ 20in (51cm) cushion pad

MATERIALS

1/8 fold set on point
Finished size:
22in (56cm) square

▲ motif fabric: 20in (51cm) square patterned or solid-coloured cotton fabric

▲ background and backing fabric: 24in (61cm) square solid black cotton fabric, plus one 23 x 14in (58.5 x 35.5cm) and one 23 x 18in (58.5 x 46cm) rectangle

▲ lining fabric: 26in (66cm) square of calico (muslin)

▲ wadding (batting): 26in (66cm) square of Hobbs Thermore or 2oz polyester wadding

▲ 3yd (2.7m) white piping cord

▲ 3yd (2.7m) bias binding

▲ 22in (56cm) square cushion pad

OTHER REQUIREMENTS

For both designs

▲ basic sewing kit

▲ appliqué and quilting needles

▲ white tacking (basting) thread

▲ sewing thread to match your motif fabric

▲ quilting thread

▲ thin card (eg a cereal box), sharp paper scissors and permanent marker

▲ HB propelling (automatic) pencil and ball-point pen

▲ quilters' clear plastic ruler, 24 x 6in

▲ rotary cutter and cutting mat

▲ masking tape

Glorious William; detail showing hand appliqué with traditional contour quilting

Dragon's Tail

Finished size:
18in (46cm) square

The red dragon on the Welsh flag represents a symbol of independence, and throughout the centuries this mythical creature has been portrayed in a variety of styles. For this design the dragon has been stylised to fit a 1/4 fold layout, with the mirror image of the curled tail forming the Welsh Heart of Love. I've used a red and green paisley-print designer fabric for the motif, and appliquéd it to a solid green background. Follow the instructions on pages 35-36 for creating the quarter-fold motif; the instructions for the appliqué, quilting and making up the cushion cover are just the same as for *New Beginnings* (see page 56). The template for this design is on page 104.

Dragon's Tail (right, and detail below); contemporary colourway, hand appliqué with traditional and contemporary contour quilting

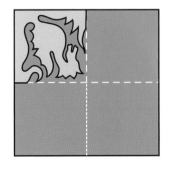
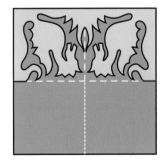

*Now you're familiar with this unique art form you can make decorative projects for the home; the two tablecloth designs and the tissue-box cover will add a fresh accent to your room accessories. The tissue-box cover and the central motif design for **Malvern Splendour** are both abstract patterns, whereas the outside edge motif for the circular tablecloth features the image of a dolphin swimming into waves. (I've used two different fabrics for the tablecloths as they pick up colour-schemes for two separate rooms, but if you want, you can economise by cutting both tablecloth motifs from one yard or metre of fabric!)*

Malvern Splendour

Finished size:
29½in (75cm) in diameter

Malvern Splendour; contemporary colourway, hand appliqué with machine and traditional contour quilting

I designed the motif for this one-sixth pattern to fit a circular tabletop measuring 19in (48.5cm) in diameter. If necessary, you can always adapt the pattern to fit the measurements of your tablecloth by either reducing or enlarging the template on a photocopier; remember that your fabric requirements will alter accordingly. As this design is a one-sixth pattern, you'll need to fold the motif and background fabric quite differently from the one-quarter and one-eighth fold designs, as explained on pages 37-41. The full-size template for this design is on page 105.

MATERIALS

▲ fabric: ¾yd (70cm), 45in (114cm) wide (this measurement includes enough fabric for 2¾yd/2.6m of 1in/2.5cm bias binding)

▲ background fabric: 2yd (1.8m) (this measurement includes enough for the background of the motif and the backing of the tablecloth)

▲ wadding (batting): 35in (89cm) square of Hobbs Thermore wadding or similar

OTHER REQUIREMENTS

▲ basic sewing kit

▲ white tacking (basting) thread

▲ appliqué and quilting needles

▲ sewing thread to match the motif

▲ quilting thread

▲ quilters' ruler

▲ compass tool (or your own version – see page 25)

▲ fabric-marking pencil in a colour that will show on your fabric

▲ protractor

▲ poster card for making template

▲ pinking shears

▲ rotary cutter and cutting mat (optional)

Making the template

1 Photocopy the motif design on page 105. Either glue the photocopy of the pattern to thin cardboard, right side uppermost, or follow the instructions for template making on page 27. Use your sharp paper scissors to cut out the cardboard template, then label the diagonal lines and centre with a permanent marker. Seam allowances are included on the template.

Preparing the motif

2 From the motif fabric cut one 23in (58.5cm) square and one 18in (46cm) square. From the background fabric cut two 35in (89cm) squares.

3 Lay the larger square of motif fabric and the smaller square of background fabric side by side on a flat surface. For each stage of the folding technique, fold one square and then the other before moving on to the next stage – this will ensure that the squares have folds and creases in the same places. Follow the instructions on pages 37-41 to create an accurate 1/6 fold in each square.

4 Place the folded background fabric to one side and work on the folded motif fabric only for the next two stages. Thread a needle with white tacking thread and tack (baste) along the diagonal lines close to the folded edge and through the central line (**A**).

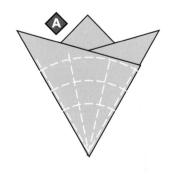

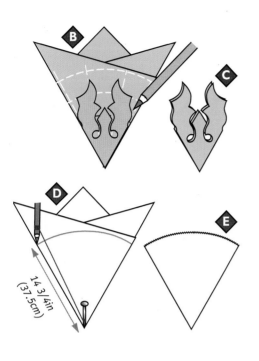

5 Position the cardboard template on the motif fabric, matching the diagonal lines, and mark around the template with a pencil (**B**). Cut out the motif shape following the pencil line and remove the tacking stitches (**C**); don't unfold the motif fabric at this stage.

TIP *I cut the outside edge of the background fabric with pinking shears to prevent them from fraying while you're appliquéing.*

6 It's much easier to cut out an accurate circle while the background fabric is still folded. Place the pin of the compass tool in the centre point of the folded background fabric, and mark an arc from one folded edge to the other (**D**). (The arc measurement is approximately 14¾in (37.5cm) from the centre point along one folded side.) Cut along the marked line with pinking shears (**E**); this prevents the raw edges from fraying as you handle the fabric during the appliqué. **Do not throw away the offcut of background fabric**.

7 Unfold the background fabric on a large, flat surface and follow the instructions on pages 39-40 for unfolding the motif fabric on top so that the creases and grooves coincide (**F-J**). Pin and tack the motif in place (see pages 33-35 for detailed instructions on pinning and tacking).

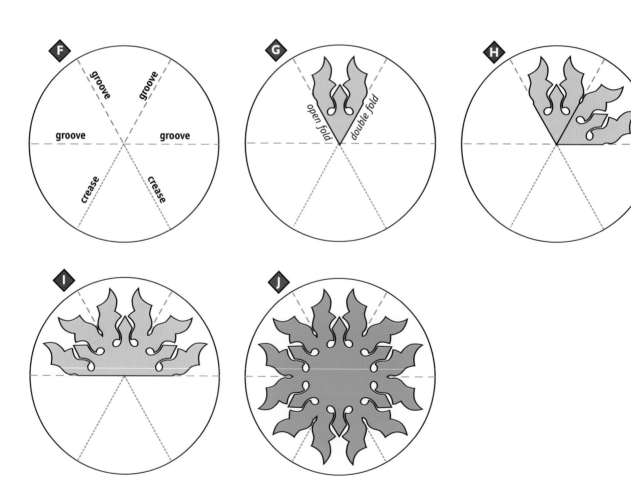

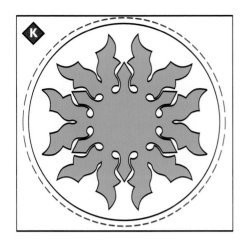

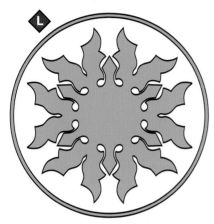

Needle turn appliqué

8 Appliqué the motif to the background fabric with toning thread (see pages 44-52 for detailed instructions on working different parts of the appliqué). When all the appliqué is complete, remove the tacking stitches and press the piece carefully with a steam iron on the reverse side of work to remove the fold lines and creases

Quilting

9 Before you sandwich the layers, reattach the background fabric offcut to the circular design by tacking it in place (**K**). This helps to prevent any distortion to the cut outside edge while you're quilting. Lay the backing square right side down and cover it with the wadding and the appliquéd motif. It's entirely your choice how you quilt the design. I've chosen to flatten the background fabric with dense contour quilting, stitching the rows ¼in (6mm) apart. The central motif has free machine quilting (vermicelli style), as I wanted to have a flat base for flower vases – you may wish to hand-quilt the motif. See page 53 for suggestions on different types of quilting.

Finishing

10 Remove the extra piece of fabric tacked round the edge, and trim the backing square and the wadding to the circular shape.

11 Follow the instructions for quick strip bias binding on page 90 to make and join the binding strips from the 18in (46cm) square of motif fabric, then use them to bind the outside of the tablecloth (**L**).

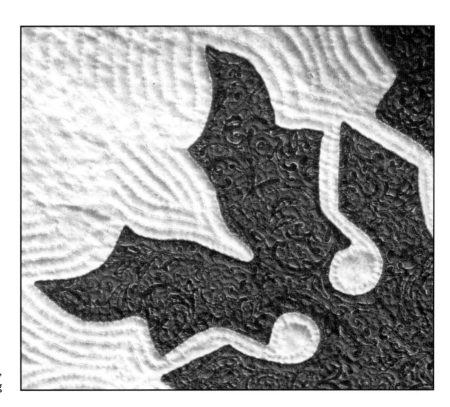

Malvern Splendour; details of hand appliqué, machine and traditional contour quilting

Ocean Blue

Finished size:
33in (84cm) in diameter

This border design gives you an alternative option for a 1/6 pattern layout. As the appliquéd border motif lies below the rim of a 19in (48.5cm) diameter table top, I have added a central contemporary element – consisting of two dolphins swimming into waves – to the traditional contour quilting. As this design is a one-sixth pattern, you'll need to fold the motif and background fabric quite differently from the one-quarter and one-eighth fold designs, as explained on pages 37-41. The template for this design is on pages 106-107.

MATERIALS

Ocean Blue; contemporary colourway, hand appliqué with traditional and contemporary contour quilting

▲ motif fabric: plain (solid) or patterned, 36in (91.5cm) square
▲ background fabric: calico (muslin), 36in (91.5cm) square
▲ lining fabric: calico (muslin), 36in (91.5cm) square

▲ wadding (batting): 36in (91.5cm) square Hobbs Thermore or 2oz polyester wadding

▲ bias binding (same fabric as motif): 3¼yd (3m) strip, 1in (2.5cm) wide

OTHER REQUIREMENTS

▲ basic sewing kit

▲ appliqué and quilting needles

▲ white tacking thread

▲ sewing thread to match your motif fabric

▲ quilting thread

▲ fabric marking pencil

▲ thin cardboard (poster card), sharp paper scissors and permanent marker

▲ HB propelling (automatic) pencil and ball-point pen

▲ quilters' clear plastic ruler, 24 x 6in

▲ masking tape

▲ compass tool (or your own version – see page 25)

▲ protractor

▲ pinking shears

▲ rotary cutter and cutting mat (optional)

Making the template

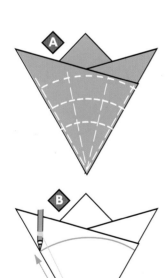

1 Photocopy the motif design on pages 106-107, enlarging it by the percentage given. Either glue the photocopy of the pattern to thin cardboard, right side uppermost, or follow the instructions for template making on page 27. Use your sharp paper scissors to cut out the cardboard template, then label the diagonal lines and the centre with a permanent marker.

Preparing the motif

2 Follow the instructions on page 37 for folding the squares of background and motif fabrics. As the large squares are difficult to fold on a narrow ironing board, I suggest you make the folds on a larger flat surface. Prepare the folded motif fabric with tacking (basting) stitches as described on page 73 (**A**).

3 It's much easier to mark and cut the circular edge on the background fabric while it's still folded. Working out from the centre fold along one side of the diagonal lines, measure 16½in (42cm), mark the spot with a pencil, and repeat the same procedure on the opposite side. Using the compass tool, draw an arc from dot to dot (**B**), and use pinking shears to cut along the marked line.

16 1/2in (42cm)

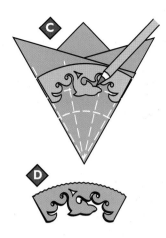

4 Place the one-sixth cardboard template onto the folded motif fabric surface, aligning both diagonal folds, and with a fabric marking pencil trace round the motif outline and the outside edge onto the motif fabric surface (**C**).

5 Remove the template. Carefully cut round the motif outline with your fabric scissors from fold to fold, and along the outside edge with a pair of pinking shears (**D**). **Don't throw away the offcut of background fabric.**

6 As we're dealing with a border design here, I'll talk you through all the stages of opening up the motif so that it ends up in exactly the right place. Open the background fabric on a flat surface, right side up, with the four grooves in the upper half of the circle (**E**). Next, lay the folded border design, wrong side up, into the middle third division, placing the open fold so that it aligns with the left diagonal line, with the cut edges of the motif and the background fabric aligning (**F**).

7 Open the first fold from left to right (**G**), then open the second fold from right to left (**H**). At this point all the folds should be aligning with the four grooves on the top half of the background fabric. Open the final fold towards you, matching the two creases in the bottom half (**I**); only now will you see the correct side of the motif fabric. Gently pat the motif into place; **don't pull it into position**.

8 Once the motif is correctly unfolded, begin pinning the motif to the background fabric along the fold lines. Then pin the inside cut edges of the motif, and finally the outsides edges. Tack (baste) in the same order – see pages 33-35 for detailed instructions on pinning and tacking.

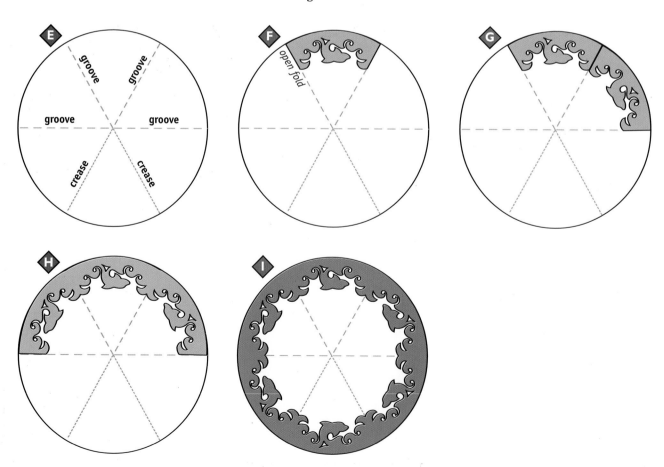

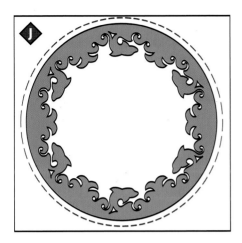

Ocean Blue; detail showing the central hand quilted design

Needle turn appliqué

9 Stitch all the inner edges of the motif to the background fabric (see pages 44-52 for detailed instructions on needle turn appliqué).

TIP *If you're going to use the dolphin quilting design, you'll find it easier if you mark the lines onto the background before pressing and sandwiching the tablecloth layers together.*

Quilting

10 Once the appliqué is complete, remove the tacking stitches and check that there are no loose threads or visible protruding threads over the appliqué line. For pressing instructions see page 52. Before you sandwich the layers together, reattach the background fabric off-cut to the circular outside edge by tacking it in place (**J**). Layer the background fabric, wadding and appliquéd design ready for quilting.

11 For this design I've covered the background fabric with dense quilting. In addition, because the border design lies below the rim of my circular table, I've added a slight variation to the central contour quilting. I've drawn an image of two dolphins swimming into waves and used this for my quilting stencil; I highlighted the outlines of the dolphins in blue quilting thread, to provide a contrast with the natural-coloured background fabric. If you'd like to use the same design, you'll find a full-size template on page 107. To blend the central and outside border designs, follow the guidelines on page 54.

Finishing

12 Remove the extra piece of fabric tacked round the edge, and trim the backing square and the wadding to the circular shape. Use the bias strip to bind the outside of the tablecloth (**K**).

Tissue Box Cover

I've worked this design to cover the largest common size for tissue boxes, but as there isn't a standard size I recommend that you check the measurements of your regular brand before you begin this project. If necessary, you can shorten the finished base edge after you've attached the ends to the main section. The full-size template for this design is on page 108.

MATERIALS

for the main section:

▲ motif fabric: 10½ x 13½in (27 x 34.5cm)

▲ contrast fabric: 10½ x 13½in (27 x 34.5cm) rectangle for the background

▲ lining: 11½in x 14½in (29 x 37cm) rectangle

▲ Hobbs wadding (batting): 11½ x 14½in (29 x 37cm) Hobbs Thermore

▲ bias binding (to tone with your motif fabric): 1½yd (1.4m) strip, 1in (2.5cm) wide

for the end panels:

▲ motif fabric: 12½ x 7½2in (32 x 19cm)

▲ lining: 12½ x 7½ in (32 x 19cm)

▲ Hobbs wadding (batting): 12½ x 7½ in (32 x 19cm)

Tissue Box Cover; contemporary colourway, hand appliqué with hand embellishment (chicken feet) and machine quilting

▼△▼△▼△▼△▼△▼△▼△▼△▼△▼△▼△▼△▼△▼

OTHER REQUIREMENTS

▲ basic sewing kit

▲ appliqué and quilting needles

▲ white tacking (basting) thread

▲ sewing thread to match your motif fabric

▲ quilting thread

▲ fabric marking pencil

▲ thin cardboard, sharp paper scissors, and permanent marker

▲ HB propelling (automatic) pencil and ball point pen

▲ quilters' clear plastic ruler, 24in x 6in

▲ rotary cutter and cutting mat

▲ masking tape

▲ tissue box 9 x 3½ x 4½ in (23 x 9 x 11.5cm)

▲ pinking shears

Making the template

1 Trace or photocopy the motif design, box end panels and oval window (aperture) on pages 108 and 109, and use these to make templates (see page 27). (For templates this small, the front and back panels of a cereal box are ideal.)

2 Using a sharp pair of paper scissors, cut out the cardboard templates. With a permanent marker label the straight fold lines, outside edges and seam allowances on the appropriate edges of the 1/4 template. Then mark the seam allowances on all the templates. Finally, draw the outline for the cutting edge on the oval window template.

TIP *For this project I used a small pair of curved manicure scissors to cut out the template.*

Preparing the motif

3 Before you begin pressing the motif fabric, mark and outline the ½in (12mm) seam allowance with a white tacking stitch (**A**). Then place both the motif and background fabric rectangles (the 10½ x 13½in/27 x 34.5cm ones) on your ironing board; lay them side by side, right side up, with their grains corresponding. Fold each of the pieces separately into a one-quarter fold (see the detailed instructions on page 35).

4 Using a coloured thread, secure the layers of the folded motif fabric with three rows of tacking stitches (**B**); start the rows ½in (12mm) in from the outside edge along all four sides, and work the rows 1in (2.5cm) apart.

5 Using the 1/4 template, mark the design onto the wrong side of the folded motif fabric with a fabric marking pencil (**C**), and cut it out (**D**).

TIP *You'll need to be extra careful as you cut round the concave and sharp points; it's quite easy to cut the tips off accidentally!*

A

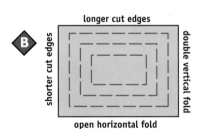
B
longer cut edges
shorter cut edges
double vertical fold
open horizontal fold

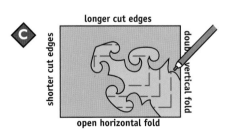
C
longer cut edges
shorter cut edges
double vertical fold
open horizontal fold

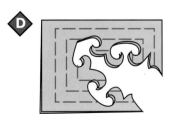
D

▼△▼△▼△▼△▼△▼△▼△▼△▼△▼△▼△▼△▼△▼

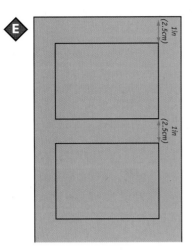

6 Next, lay the fabric for the ends of the cover (the 12½ x 7½in/32 x 19cm rectangle of motif fabric) right side up on a flat surface. Place the end template onto the surface of the fabric 1in (2.5cm) in from the top outside edge. With a fabric marking pencil trace round the outline of the template onto the right side of the motif fabric. Move the template down, allowing 1in (2.5cm) between the shapes, and mark the second outline onto the motif fabric surface (**E**). Remove the template and place the marked end fabric to one side.

7 Lay the open background fabric on a flat surface, right side up, with the vertical groove in the top half (**F**). Remove the tacking threads from the folded motif and lay the motif in the upper left quadrant of the background fabric, aligning the double fold with the vertical groove and the open fold with the central horizontal groove (**G**). Open the motif fabric from left to right so that the horizontal fold of the motif rests in the central horizontal groove (**H**). Then open the motif fabric towards you to reveal the right side, matching the vertical crease with the vertical crease in the background fabric (**I**).

8 Pin and tack the motif in place (for guidelines on tacking follow the instructions on pages 34-35).

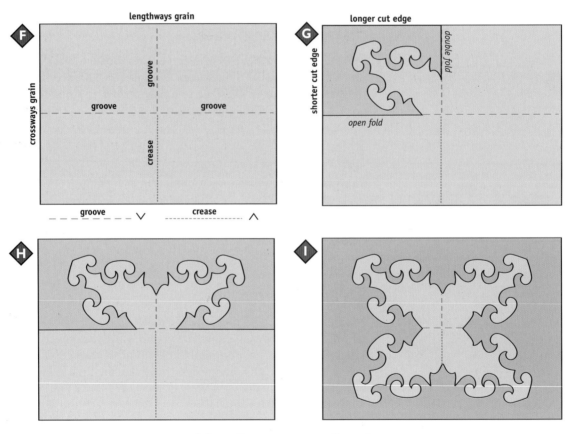

Needle turn appliqué

9 Although this is a miniature piece of work the turning allowance remains at ⅛in (3mm) on the motif edge. Appliqué the turned motif edge to the background fabric with matching thread, following the comprehensive instructions on pages 44-52. Once you've completed the appliqué, remove the tacking stitches and follow the instructions on page 52 for pressing the design. For my design, I added a line of the traditional embellishment known as *wawae moa* to the finished appliquéd edge, using a gold thread. If you'd like to do the same, you'll find detailed instructions and diagrams on page 52.

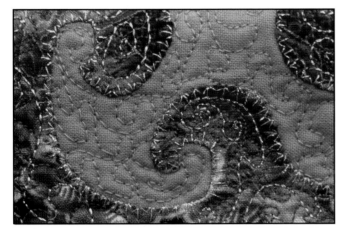

Tissue Box Cover; details showing hand appliqué and chicken feet embellishments (above left),
and machine quilting on the end of the cover (above right)

Quilting

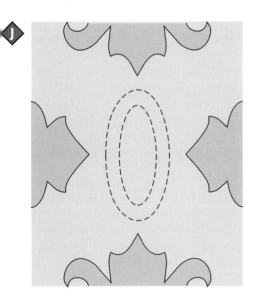

10 Before you layer the fabrics ready for quilting, use the oval window template to mark the opening (aperture) onto the top layer of the background fabric. There are two different ways of finishing the window opening at the top of the box. I bound the oval edge with bias binding (see page 90) after I'd completed the machine quilting; if you want to finish the opening with a bound edge, draw on the larger oval (marked on your master template) as well. Then work the quilting, and once the quilting is completed, move on to step 13a.

If you prefer you can simply turn under the seam allowance and blind hem it. For a turned edge, make sure that you've drawn both the smaller and larger oval lines (marked on the master template) onto the background surface (**J**) before quilting by hand or machine; tack around the larger oval line as a guide for the turned edge. Continue with the quilting as described in step 12. Once all the quilting has been completed, move on to step 13b.

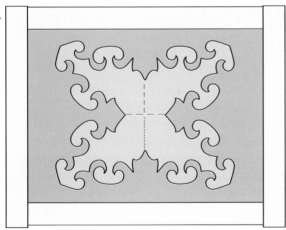

TIP *To prevent distortion of the outside edge and to help maintain an accurate overall measurement during the quilting phase I attached a 1¹/₂in (4cm) strip of calico to each side of the appliquéd top (**K**).*

11 Place the lining for the tissue box cover wrong side up on a flat surface; lay the wadding (batting) on top of the lining, checking that the edges all align. Then lay the pressed appliqué top, right side up, in the middle of the wadding so that the calico strips align with the outside edges. Next, sandwich together the end panel fabric with the wadding and lining material ready for quilting. For pieces this small I recommend that you tack (baste) the layers together before you begin quilting.

12 Work your chosen quilting design by hand or machine. As always, you decide on whether you quilt by hand or machine; you may like to experiment rather than following the traditional technique (see page 53). I chose machine quilting for this project but changed the thread to match the background and motif fabric – making sure that I didn't quilt over the marked opening line. Then to complement the simple vermicelli machine quilting I highlighted the whole motif surface with a gold thread, in particular the tigers' features on the motif fabric on the end panels.

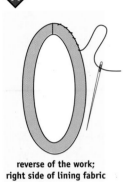

right side of
background fabric

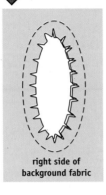

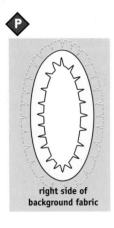

reverse of the work;
right side of lining fabric

right side of
background fabric

right side of
background fabric

reverse of the work;
right side of lining fabric

Finishing

13a *For a bound opening* Trim the background and lining fabrics along the marked line (**L**). Before you attach the binding, trim one angled end of the binding strip, then turn under and press a ¼in (6mm) seam allowance. Place the folded end against the background fabric, starting at the top of the oval window arc; sew in place with a ¼in (6mm) seam allowance (**M**). To join the ends of the bias binding, overlap the straight turned edge by ¼in (6mm); turn the binding over the cut fabric edge and hem it to the inside surface of the lining fabric (**N**).

13b *For a hemmed opening* Cut along the inner outline of the marked oval window with a sharp pair of fabric scissors. Before turning the edge under, you'll need first to clip the inner window edge with ⅛in (3mm) cuts at regular intervals (**O**). Fold the edges of the background fabric under by ¼in (6mm) and finger-press them at regular intervals (**P**). Then work from the reverse side; turn the lining fabric under a generous ¼in (6-7mm), so that the turned edge is concealed under the folded rim of the background fabric; hem in place (**Q**).

14 Remove the four calico strips from the outside edge of the appliquéd top, and lay the design on your cutting mat. Using a clear plastic ruler and a rotary cutter, trim away the excess wadding to leave an accurate 12½ x 10in (32 x 25.5cm) rectangle. Then cut out the two end panels accurately (they measure 4⅝ x 5½in/11.75 x 14cm).

15 With the right sides together, attach the end panels of the cover to the main section. Pin and tack each section in place along the ½in (12mm) seam allowance line (**R**) before machining. Before stitching each stage, slip the cover over the tissue box to make sure it fits; if not, adjust the seams appropriately.

16 Next, stitch along the tacked seam allowance, easing and adjusting the corners as needed. With a pair of pinking shears trim the inside seam allowance back to a generous ¼in (6mm), and clip the corners wherever necessary to make them lie flat.

17 Slip the cover over the tissue box so that you can mark the finished base line; trim to length. Attach the binding to the edge of the base with the side seams pressed closed, towards the side panels. Turn the binding over the raw edges, then pin, tack and hem it to the inside surface of the lining fabric. Finally, turn the cover right side out and place it over the tissue box.

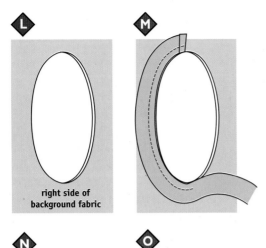

main section:
right side of
lining fabric

main section:
right side of appliquéd motif

tacking line

side panel:
wrong side of
motif fabric

Anthurium Wall-Hanging

Finished size:
43in (109.5cm) square

For generations Hawaiian quilters have used the heart-shaped petal of the anthurium as their design resource for appliqué motifs. The plant was brought to the islands in 1899 by Samuel Damon, an English missionary. I designed the contemporary pattern for this wall-hanging using the negative space of a right-angled triangle, which creates a circular pattern without having to fold your fabric into a one-sixth fold first (the usual way of creating a circular design). I used a slightly patterned fabric as my background, but any cotton fabric, or something like unbleached calico (muslin), would work well. The templates for this design are on pages 110-111.

Anthurium Wall-Hanging; contemporary colourway, hand appliqué with traditional and contemporary contour quilting

Anthurium Wall-Hanging; detail showing hand appliqué with traditional and contemporary contour quilting

Materials

▲ motif fabric: 2yd (2m) cotton fabric (this measurement includes enough fabric for 5½yd/5m of bias binding for the wall-hanging)

▲ background fabric: 44in (112cm) square of contrasting cotton fabric

▲ lining fabric: 48in (122cm) square of calico (muslin) for backing your quilt 'sandwich'

▲ wadding (batting): 48in (122cm) square of Hobbs Thermore or 2oz polyester wadding

Other requirements

▲ basic sewing kit

▲ appliqué and quilting needles

▲ white tacking (basting) thread

▲ sewing thread to match your motif fabric

▲ quilting thread

▲ fabric-marking pencil (white or yellow)

▲ thin card (A2 sheet of poster card), sharp paper scissors and permanent marker

▲ HB propelling pencil and ball-point pen

▲ quilters' clear plastic ruler, 24 x 6in

▲ rotary cutter and cutting mat

▲ masking tape

Making the template

1 Photocopy the designs on pages110-111, enlarging them by the percentage marked beside the templates, then use the pattern to mark (**A**) and cut out (**B**) a pair of cardboard templates. Use a sharp pair of paper scissors to cut out the two cardboard templates; with a permanent marker label the centre, diagonal and straight lines on the appropriate outside edges of the motif template, then mark the cut outside edge, diagonal and straight lines on the separate border template.

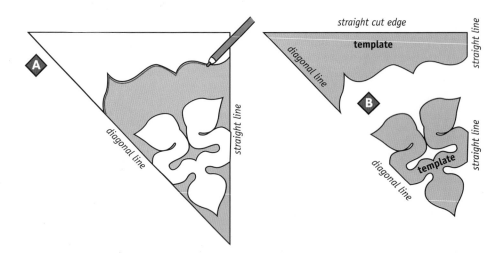

Cutting the fabric

2 From the motif fabric, cut one 44in (112cm) square for the appliqué motif and one 26in (66cm) square for the bias binding.

Preparing the motif

With a project of this size it's impossible to fit both squares of fabric side by side onto your ironing board. You'll find it much easier to fold the fabric squares in half first on the table; then carefully lift one piece at a time onto your ironing board to continue the folding and pressing. As the design has a border incorporated into the pattern, the outside cut edges must align perfectly in order to ensure that the design element is the same depth on all sides. You'll also need to add extra rows of horizontal tacking (basting) along the cut outside edge (see pages 30-31 for tips on folding, pressing and tacking).

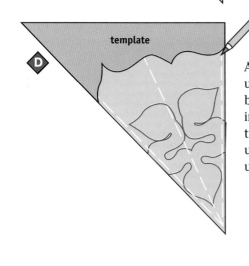

3 First lay the 1/8 cardboard template onto the folded and tacked motif fabric, aligning the diagonal and straight marked edges with the folded fabric; using a fabric-marking pencil, draw round the motif outline onto the motif fabric surface (**C**). Then remove the motif template. Next, lay the card template for the border onto the motif fabric, aligning the diagonal, straight and outside cut edges; again using a fabric-marking pencil, draw round the border outline onto the motif fabric surface (**D**). (See page 32 for full instructions and diagrams for marking.)

4 With a sharp pair of fabric scissors, carefully cut out the folded border and motif along the marked lines (**E**); remember to leave the connectors on the diagonal and straight folds intact so that you end up with the correct repeat pattern when the fabric is unfolded. (See page 32 for hints on cutting out the motif.) Although you'll find it easier to unfold the central motif and the border design separately, as explained in step 5 on page 88, I've combined the two separate sections of the pattern in the unfolding sequence below to avoid unnecessary repetition.

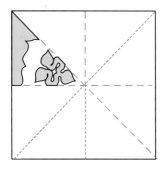 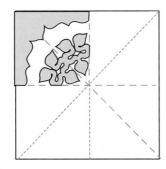 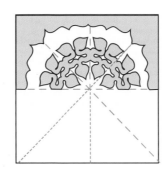

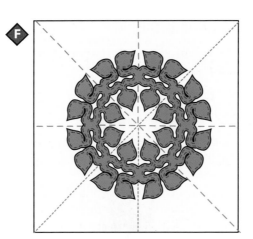

5 As there are two separate elements to this pattern, it's much easier to unfold the central motif onto the background fabric first. Then pin and tack this onto the background (**F**) before unfolding, pinning and tacking the border motif onto the background (**G**). Refer back to pages 32-35 for specific instructions on unfolding, pinning and tacking.

TIP *Before you begin any appliqué, outline the finished size on the wrong side of the background fabric and tack along the marked line. This gives you a guideline for trimming the surplus lining and wadding at step 10.*

Needle turn appliqué

6 Once the two pieces of motif fabric are tacked into place, remove the pins and begin appliquéing the turned motif edge to the background fabric, starting from the centre and working out towards the border. (See pages 44-52 for the comprehensive instructions and diagrams on the basic technique, finger pressing, points and Vs.) In the detail of the wall-hanging (*right*) you can see the appliquéd edges of the main motif.

Quilting

7 Before you begin any quilting, follow the suggestions on pages 52 and 53 for preparing and pressing the quilt top.

8 As this is quite a large project you may prefer to sandwich the layers together on the floor. First lay the lining down, wrong side up, then position the wadding on top so that the edges align. Now lay the pressed appliqué top in the middle of the wadding, right side up, so that there's a 2in (5cm) border of wadding all the way around (**H**). Use your favourite method (see page 53) to secure the layers of your quilt sandwich.

9 You now have various choices. The thread used for traditional quilting is white or ecru, but you may want to add colour as I've done – I chose to outline the edge of the motif, and to quilt the appliqué design, with blue quilting thread. You may wish to use a contemporary quilting pattern for the motif and border, or to continue with the traditional technique of echo quilting (see page 53). If you do use echo quilting, you'll need to use blending (see page 54) to harmonise the two shapes (**I**, **J** and **K**).

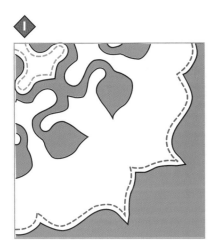  

Finishing

10 Before you straighten the outside edges of the quilted top, remove any tacking stitches. Place the quilted top on a flat surface, right side up, and trim the design; follow the instructions on page 93 for binding the edges (**L**), and the instructions on page 94 for attaching a hanging sleeve.

TIP *To prevent the quilt from moving out of position while you're trimming the edges, place a pile of books along the middle of the quilted top.*

Anthurium Wall-Hanging; detail showing hand appliqué with traditional and contemporary contour quilting

Finishing techniques

Bias binding

We all have our own special methods for making bias binding. Personally I find the technique which involves making a tube of continuous bias (out of a parallelogram of fabric) both difficult and time-consuming, and also frustrating when the lines don't meet! There is a much simpler method, which involves little effort with perfect end results.

First of all, you need to determine the width of the bias required for binding your project. For example, piped cording round a cushion (pillow) will require bias strips 1½in (4cm) wide to cover the cord (possibly slightly more or less, depending on the width of the cording). In contrast, for binding the outside edge of the tablecloth, or the window opening (aperture) or base of the tissue box cover, you'll need strips of bias binding that are 1in (2.5cm) wide. For binding the outside edge of the wall-hanging you'll need strips 2¼in (5.5cm) wide.

To determine the quantity of binding required, first measure the perimeter or circumference of the unfinished project edge. For example, to add piped cording to a square cushion cover with a finished size of 18in (46cm): the unfinished cushion front will measure 19in (48.5cm) square, giving you a perimeter of 76in (193cm). Therefore, you'll need approximately 2½yd (2.3m) of binding – this measurement allows a little extra for the piped corners and joins.

Even though the tissue box cover (see page 80) is a relatively small project, the base has a 28in (71cm) perimeter, and the oval window opening (aperture) measures 8in (20.5cm) in circumference. Depending on how you choose to finish the window opening, the total binding requirement for this project could be as much as 1½yd (1.4m).

The two circular tablecloths have different circumferences. *Malvern Splendour* (see page 72) has a circumference of 90in (228.5cm), requiring 2¾yd (2.5m) of binding, while the circumference of *Ocean Blue* (see page 76) is 105½in (268cm), so needing 3¼yd (nearly 3m) of binding. The amounts of binding I've suggested include an allowance for joins.

Finally, the perimeter of the Anthurium wall-hanging (see page 85) measures 172in (437cm), which means a requirement of 5½yd (around 5m) of binding. This includes an extra allowance for mitred corners and joins.

Quick strip bias binding

It's useful to know how to make your own bias binding, as then you can match the binding to your appliquéd motif. This is a very quick and easy technique for cutting bias strips without wasting too much fabric. For example, to add piped cording to a square 19in (48.5cm) cushion front panel, you only need to start with an 18in (46cm) square of fabric.

1 Fold a square of fabric in half diagonally (**A**) and then in half diagonally again (**B**). Press each new fold carefully to avoid any distortion along the diagonal fold line.

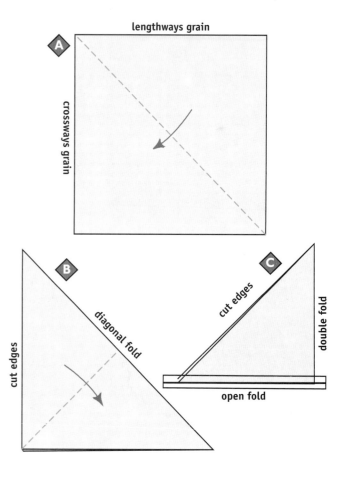

2 Use a rotary cutter, clear plastic quilters' ruler and cutting mat for the next stage; place the ruler over the folded edge and cut 1½in (4cm) wide bias strips (**C**). (You may need to alter the width of the strips depending on the precise project you're working on.) The first cut strip will be double; cut along its fold line to separate the strips.

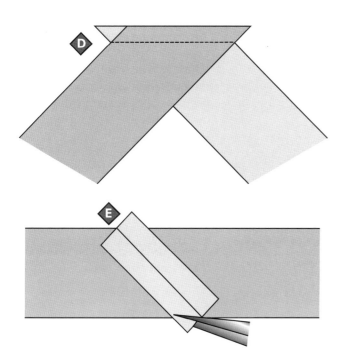

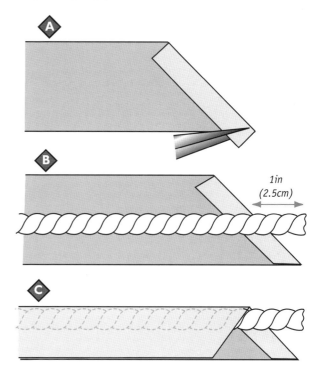

Piped cording

Piping adds a lovely finishing touch to projects such as cushion (pillow) covers; it can work very well if you use the same fabric for the piping as you've used for the appliqué motif.

1 Before you begin covering the cord, fold the diagonal end of the binding strip under by ½in (12mm) and trim off the excess fabric that protrudes over the straight edge (**A**). Lay the cord on the wrong side of the bias strip, 1in (2.5cm) over the cut end (**B**). Fold the fabric over the cord, aligning the long straight edges (**C**).

3 Join the strips together using cross-way seams (**D**); press the seams open and trim the extended triangles level with the cut edge of the bias strip (**E**).

Adding binding

> **TIP** *I find that it's much easier to turn, trim and press an angled seam allowance to the end of the bias binding strip before I begin to apply it.*

1 Pin the binding to the front of the work, aligning the raw edges (**A**), and stitch in place.

2 Fold the excess over to the back of the work, folding under the raw edge of the binding; pin it in position and secure with a blind hemming stitch (**B**).

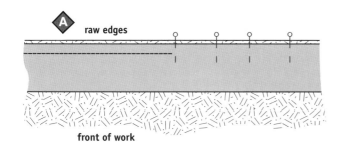

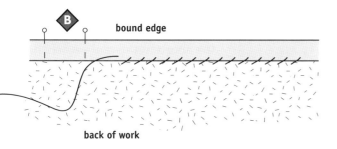

2 Set your sewing machine stitch length to approximately 3.5 (the length used for tacking). Use your left hand to hold the cord against the folded strip, and hold the long edges together with your right hand, making sure that they stay aligned. To allow you to join the cording later if you need to (see step 6), begin stitching 2½in (6.5cm) in from the start of the cord; sew down the complete length of the folded strip (**D**).

> **TIP** *I use a conventional machine foot for tacking the binding over the cord, but some people find a zipper foot useful to help them keep close to the piping cord.*

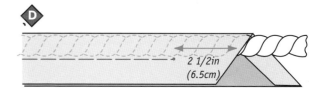

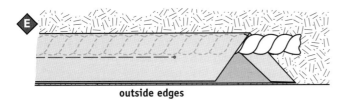

outside edges

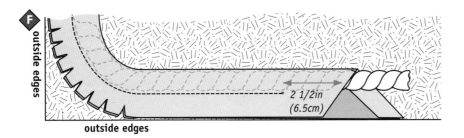

outside edges

2 1/2in
(6.5cm)

outside edges

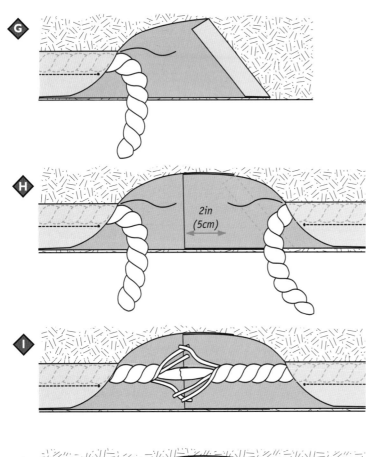

2in
(5cm)

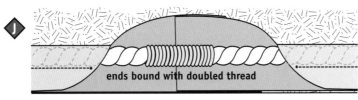

ends bound with doubled thread

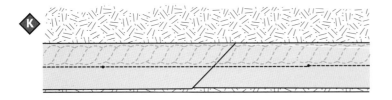

3 Begin roughly 9in (23cm) in from one corner, and lay the covered cord on the right side of your cushion front, aligning all the cut edges (**E**). Once again begin 2½in (6.5cm) in from the open end of the binding, and stitch by machine using a ½in (12mm) seam allowance. Work clockwise round the cover. Stop 2in (5cm) away from each corner and carefully clip the edges of the piping before you continue; this will help you to manipulate the piping into a curved arch round the corner (**F**).

4 Carry on stitching in the same way until you're about 2in (5cm) away from the starting point; work a few reverse stitches with the machine to secure the end of your stitching line, and cut the threads (**G**). For the next step it's much easier to remove your work from under the sewing machine foot.

5 The easiest method for joining the two bias strips where they meet is to overlap the angled edge by 2in (5cm), as shown in **H**; sew in place in the usual way, but with one layer inside the other.

TIP *At this point I blind-hem the turned edges together; it's much easier doing this now than when the fabric strip is finally wrapped round the joined cords!*

6 To join the cords, you'll need to trim both ends so that they will overlap by 1½in (4cm). Untwist each end a little, and trim one strand from each side so that their ends touch, while the remaining strands overlap (**I**). Rewrap the longer strands round the shorter ones and secure them with several hand stitches (**J**). Then fold the strip of binding over the joined cord and sew the final section of the piping in place (**K**).

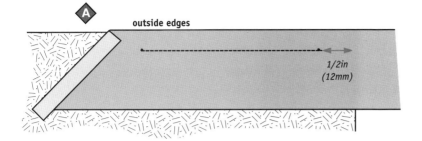

outside edges

1/2in
(12mm)

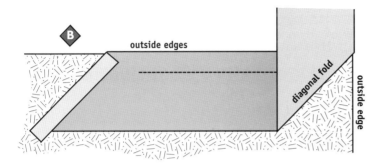

outside edges

diagonal fold

outside edge

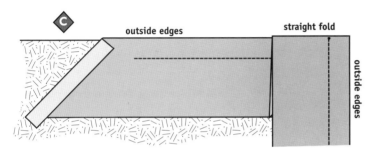

outside edges

straight fold

outside edges

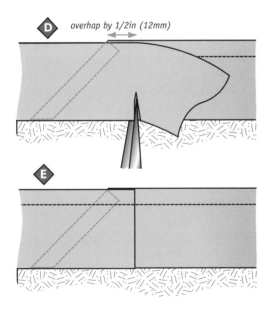

overhap by 1/2in (12mm)

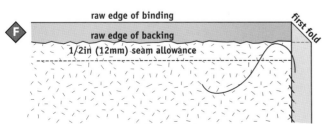

raw edge of binding

raw edge of backing

1/2in (12mm) seam allowance

first fold

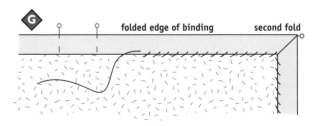

folded edge of binding

second fold

Binding edges and mitring corners

1 Sew your chosen binding to the front of your wall-hanging, using a ½in (12mm) seam allowance and stitching through all the layers. Begin 1½in (4cm) in from the cut end of the binding to allow for a join, and stop ½in (12mm) away from the corner (**A**); work a few reverse stitches with your machine before cutting the threads.

2 To mitre the corner, turn the wall-hanging around so that you can stitch along the next edge. Fold the binding up and away from you (**B**) – this automatically creates a diagonal pleat – then fold it towards you again. This positions the binding perfectly along the next edge of the wall-hanging (**C**). Begin stitching at the top of the folded edge and stitch to the next corner seam allowance. Repeat steps 1 and 2 for the next three corners.

3 To join the ends of the binding strip, overlap the angled end by ½in (12mm); clip off the excess (**D**). Continue sewing in the same way, with one end of the binding inside the other (**E**).

4 Fold the binding over the raw edges onto the back of the wall hanging, and with a matching thread, hand-stitch the edge of the binding to the backing fabric. As you reach each corner, mitre it in two easy steps. First of all, fold a diagonal pleat away from you (**F**). Place a pin in the corner as shown, then fold the binding back towards you to complete the mitre (**G**); continue sewing.

Envelope closure for cushions

I find an envelope closure the easiest method for finishing a cushion cover.

1 Measure the perimeter of the square front panel. For an 18in (46cm) cushion (19in/48.5cm square unfinished size) you'll need to cut one 19 x 14½in (48.5 x 37cm) rectangle and one 19 x 10½in (48.5 x 27cm) rectangle of fabric.

2 On one long edge of each piece, turn under and stitch a double ½in (12mm) hem allowance (**A**). The measurements are now 19 x 13½in (48.5 x 34.5cm) and 19 x 9½in (48.5 x 24cm). This will produce an overlap of 4in (10cm) on the back of the cover.

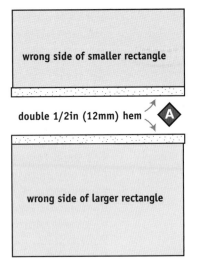

wrong side of smaller rectangle

double 1/2in (12mm) hem 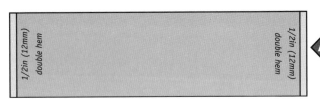 **A**

wrong side of larger rectangle

3 Lay the cushion front on a flat surface, right side up, then lay the smaller piece of backing fabric, wrong side up, on top, aligning all the raw edges. Pin, tack (baste) and sew the first piece of backing in place (**B**), taking a ½in (12mm) seam allowance.

1/2in (12mm) seam allowance **B**

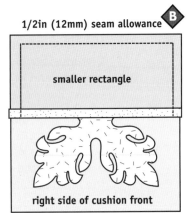

smaller rectangle

right side of cushion front

4 Lay the larger piece of backing fabric, wrong side up, on top of the first piece, aligning all the cut edges (**C**); the two sections now overlap. Pin, tack and sew this piece in place, taking a ½in (12mm) seam allowance. Trim the corners and turn the cushion cover inside out, then insert the cushion pad.

C

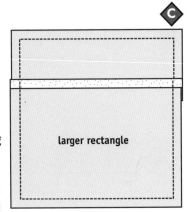

larger rectangle

Sleeve attachment for a wall-hanging

There are many different methods for making sleeve attachments; since 2001 I've been following Jenny Last's instructions for making sleeves. This technique certainly improves the way your quilt hangs against a wall, or when it's suspended from a frame.

1 Cut a strip of backing fabric 9in (23cm) wide x 44in (112cm) long. I prefer to use the same material as the backing fabric so that the sleeve blends in with the back of the quilt. Turn under and press a double ½in (12mm) hem on each shorter edge, then stitch a narrow hem (**A**).

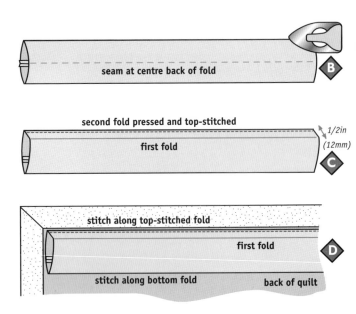

1/2in (12mm) double hem

1/2in (12mm) double hem

A

2 Fold the fabric strip in half along its length, right sides together, and stitch a ½in (12mm) seam along the level cut edges. Remove the work from your sewing machine, and cut any loose threads before turning the tube right side out.

3 Place the stitched tube on the surface of your ironing board, and press it flat so that the seam lies in the centre of the back of the tube (**B**). To help the sleeve accommodate a pole or a baton neatly, press a second crease ½in (12mm) in from one of the two long folds; to maintain this creased edge I run a line of top-stitching immediately below the new fold (**C**).

4 Pin the sleeve to the back of the wall-hanging just below the binding. Blind hem along the bottom crease, the new top-stitched creased fold and the inner edge of each end to form a tube on the back of the quilt (**D**).

seam at centre back of fold **B**

second fold pressed and top-stitched

first fold

1/2in (12mm)

C

stitch along top-stitched fold

first fold

D

stitch along bottom fold

back of quilt

Templates

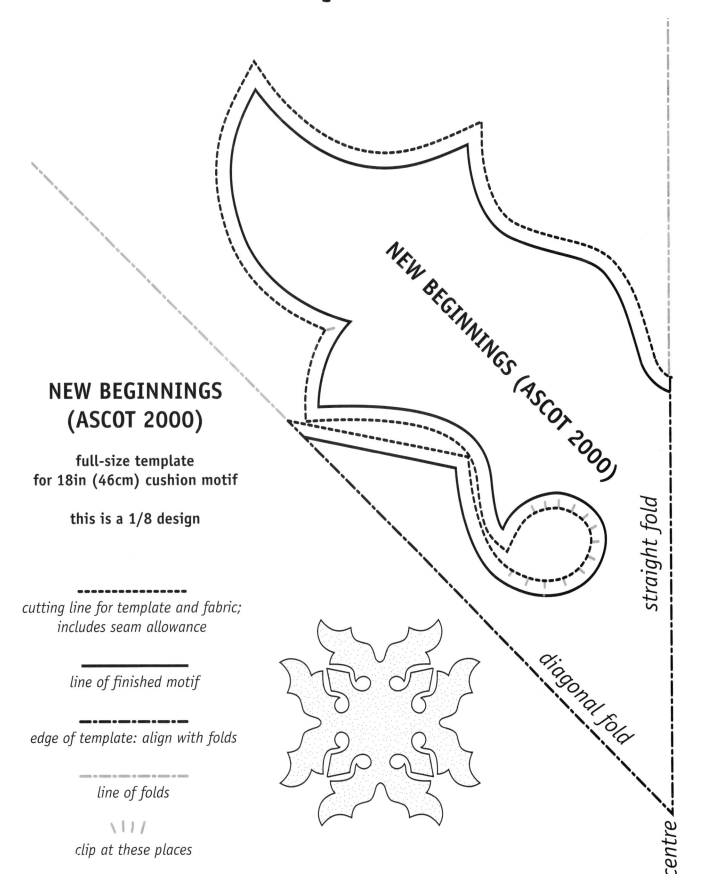

NEW BEGINNINGS (ASCOT 2000)

NEW BEGINNINGS (ASCOT 2000)

**full-size template
for 18in (46cm) cushion motif**

this is a 1/8 design

- - - - - - - - - - -
*cutting line for template and fabric;
includes seam allowance*

───────────
line of finished motif

─·─·─·─·─·─
edge of template: align with folds

─ ─ ─ ─ ─ ─
line of folds

\ | | /
clip at these places

straight fold

diagonal fold

centre

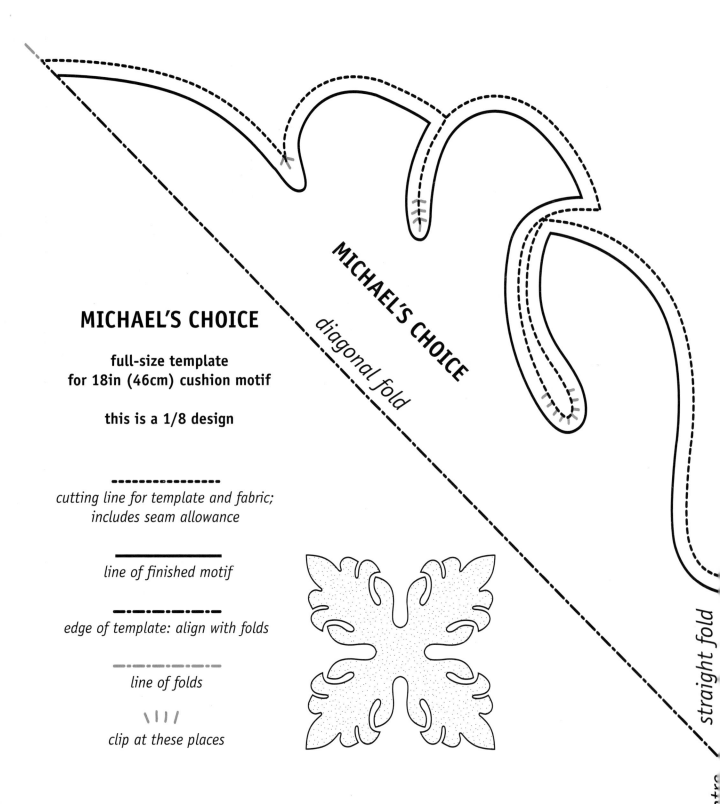

MICHAEL'S CHOICE

MICHAEL'S CHOICE

diagonal fold

straight fold

**full-size template
for 18in (46cm) cushion motif**

this is a 1/8 design

----

*cutting line for template and fabric;
includes seam allowance*

————————

line of finished motif

—·—·—·—·—·—

edge of template: align with folds

—·—·—·—·—·—

line of folds

\ | | /

clip at these places

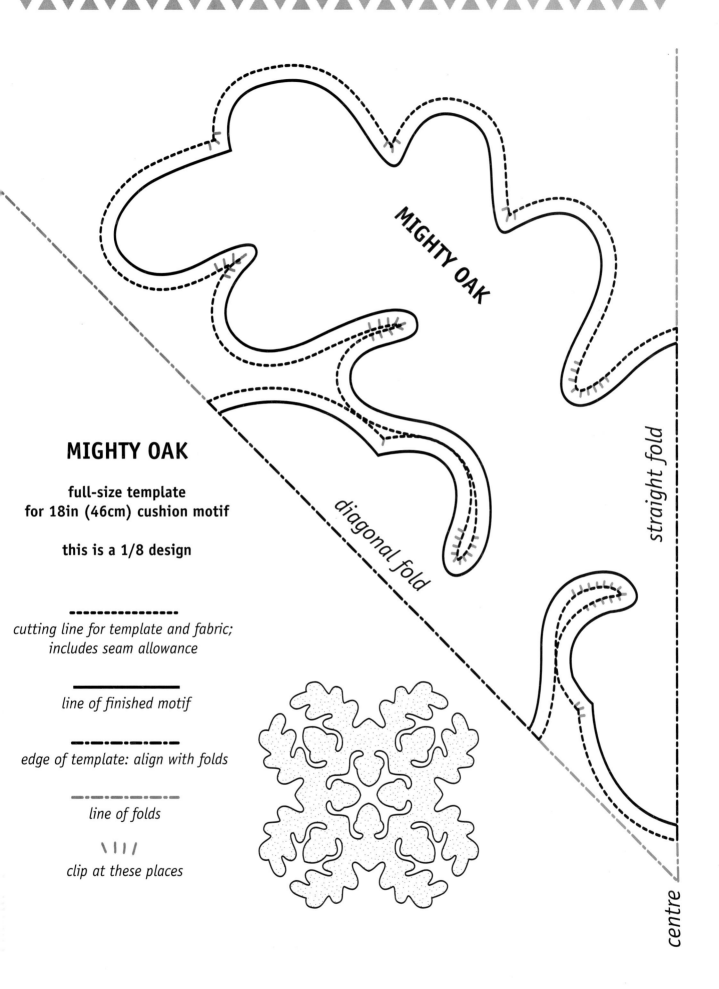

MIGHTY OAK

MIGHTY OAK

**full-size template
for 18in (46cm) cushion motif**

this is a 1/8 design

·················
*cutting line for template and fabric;
includes seam allowance*

──────
line of finished motif

▬·▬·▬·▬·
edge of template: align with folds

▬·▬·▬·▬·
line of folds

\ l l /
clip at these places

diagonal fold

straight fold

centre

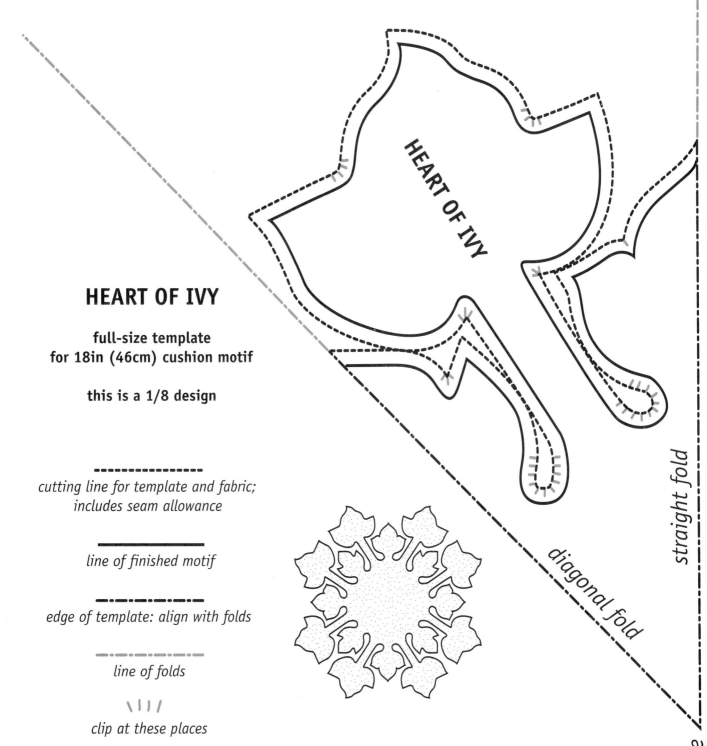

HEART OF IVY

**full-size template
for 18in (46cm) cushion motif**

this is a 1/8 design

HEART OF IVY

*cutting line for template and fabric;
includes seam allowance*

line of finished motif

edge of template: align with folds

line of folds

\ | | /

clip at these places

straight fold

diagonal fold

centre

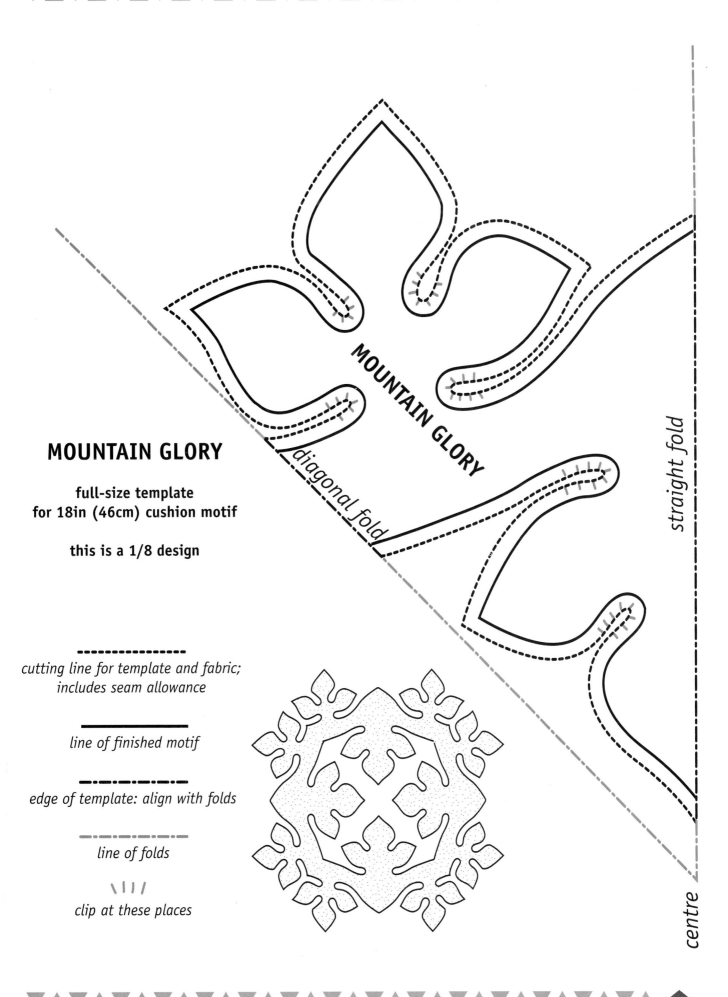

MOUNTAIN GLORY

**full-size template
for 18in (46cm) cushion motif**

this is a 1/8 design

MOUNTAIN GLORY

diagonal fold

straight fold

centre

- - - - - - - - - - - - - -
*cutting line for template and fabric;
includes seam allowance*

—————————
line of finished motif

—·—·—·—·—·—
edge of template: align with folds

—·—·—·—·—·—
line of folds

\ | | /
clip at these places

CHRISTMAS ROSE

straight fold

diagonal fold

CHRISTMAS ROSE

**full-size template
for 18in (46cm) cushion motif**

this is a 1/8 design

- - - - - - - - - - - - - - - -

*cutting line for template and fabric;
includes seam allowance*

────────────

line of finished motif

─ · ─ · ─ · ─ · ─ · ─

edge of template: align with folds

─ · · ─ · · ─ · · ─ · · ─

line of folds

\ | | |

clip at these places

centre

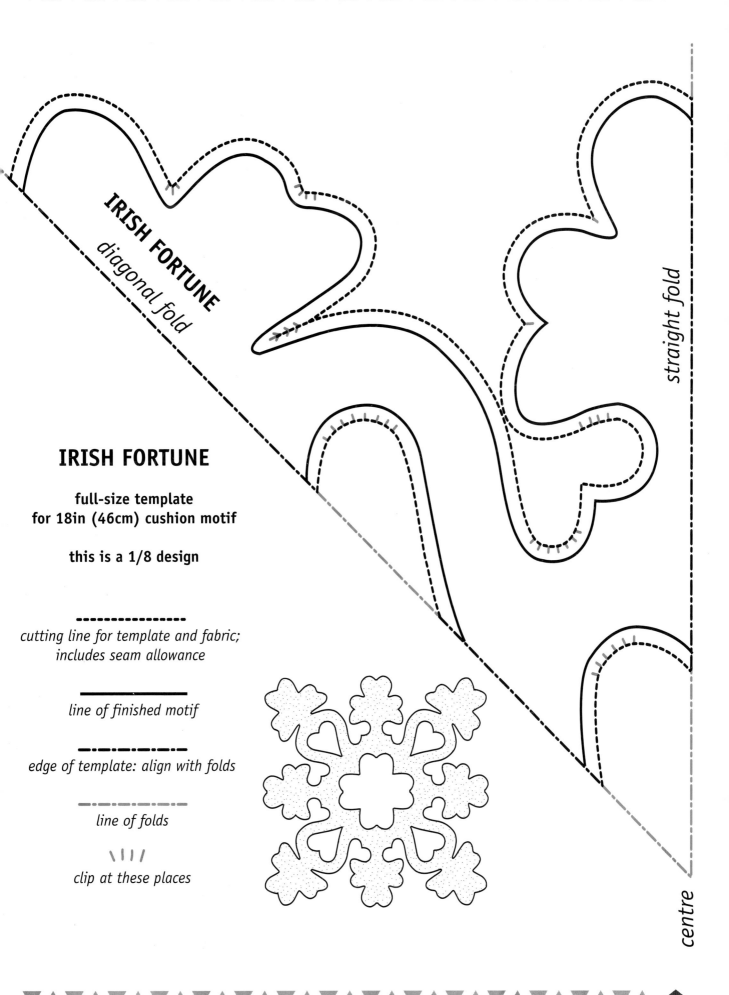

IRISH FORTUNE

diagonal fold

straight fold

IRISH FORTUNE

**full-size template
for 18in (46cm) cushion motif**

this is a 1/8 design

----

*cutting line for template and fabric;
includes seam allowance*

————————

line of finished motif

—·—·—·—·—

edge of template: align with folds

—·—·—·—·—

line of folds

\ \ / /

clip at these places

centre

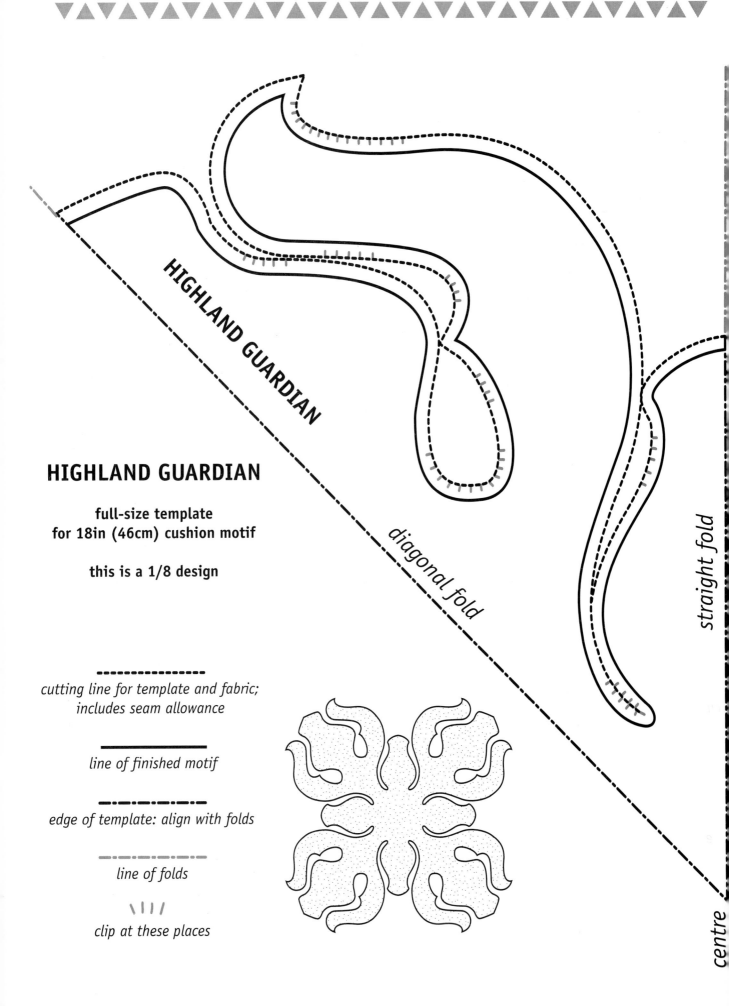

HIGHLAND GUARDIAN

diagonal fold

straight fold

centre

HIGHLAND GUARDIAN

**full-size template
for 18in (46cm) cushion motif**

this is a 1/8 design

- - - - - - - - - - - - -
*cutting line for template and fabric;
includes seam allowance*

————————
line of finished motif

— - — - — - — - —
edge of template: align with folds

- - - - - - - - - - - - -
line of folds

\ | | /
clip at these places

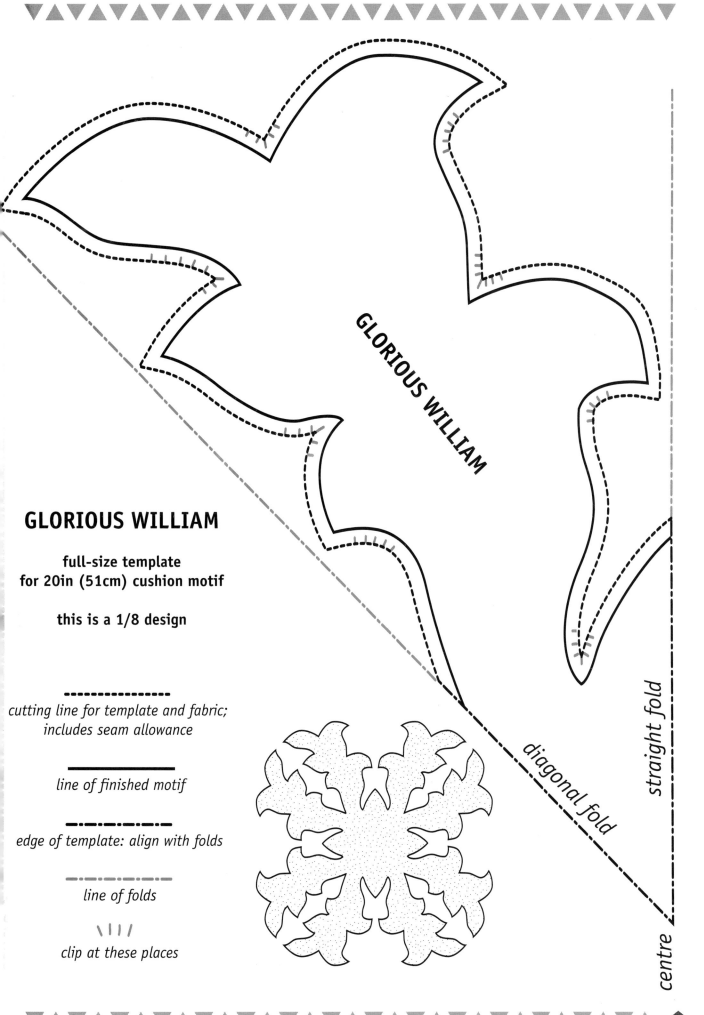

GLORIOUS WILLIAM

GLORIOUS WILLIAM

**full-size template
for 20in (51cm) cushion motif**

this is a 1/8 design

- - - - - - - - - - - - - - -

*cutting line for template and fabric;
includes seam allowance*

―――――――――

line of finished motif

▬ ▬ ▬ ▬ ▬ ▬

edge of template: align with folds

— ▪ — ▪ — ▪ — ▪ —

line of folds

\ | | /

clip at these places

diagonal fold

straight fold

centre

cut edges

vertical fold

cut edges

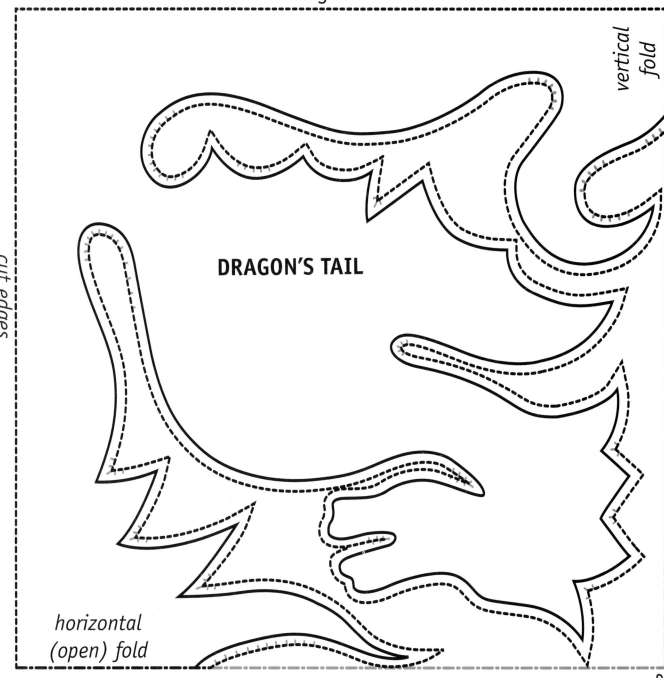

DRAGON'S TAIL

horizontal (open) fold

centre

DRAGON'S TAIL

**Enlarge by 138%
for 18in (46cm) cushion motif**

this is a 1/4 design

▬▬▬▬▬▬▬▬▬▬
*cutting line for template and fabric;
includes seam allowance*

▬▬▬▬▬
line of finished motif

▬·▬·▬·▬·▬
edge of template: align with folds

▬·▬·▬·▬·▬
line of folds

\ | | /
clip at these places

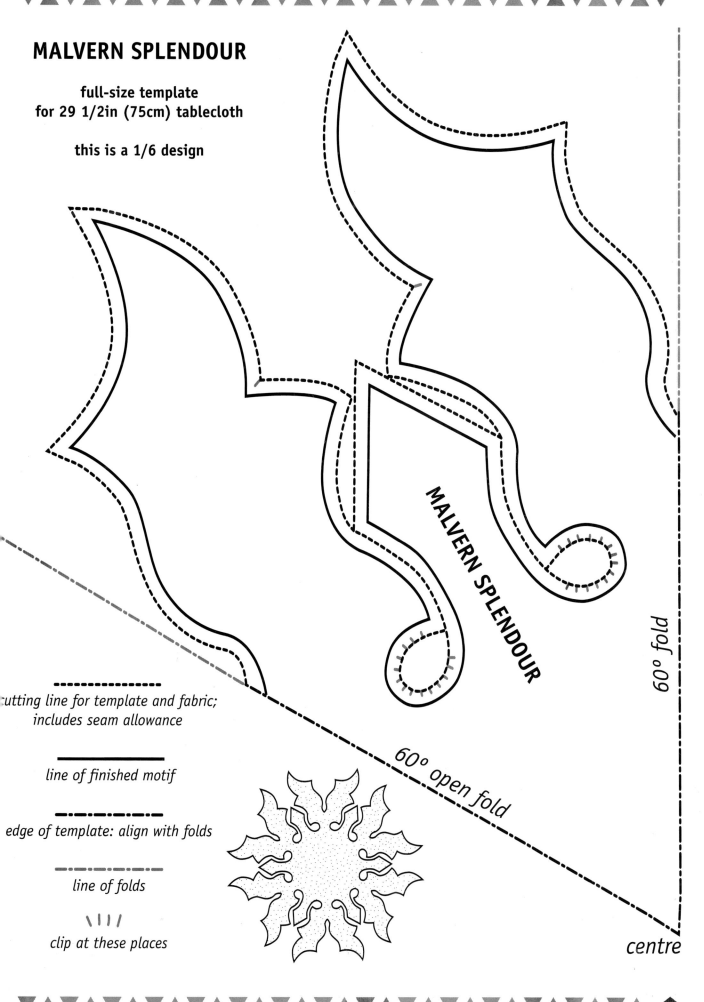

MALVERN SPLENDOUR

**full-size template
for 29 1/2in (75cm) tablecloth**

this is a 1/6 design

MALVERN SPLENDOUR

60° fold

60° open fold

centre

- - - - - - - - - -
*cutting line for template and fabric;
includes seam allowance*

─────
line of finished motif

─ · ─ · ─
edge of template: align with folds

─ · ─ · ─
line of folds

\ l l /
clip at these places

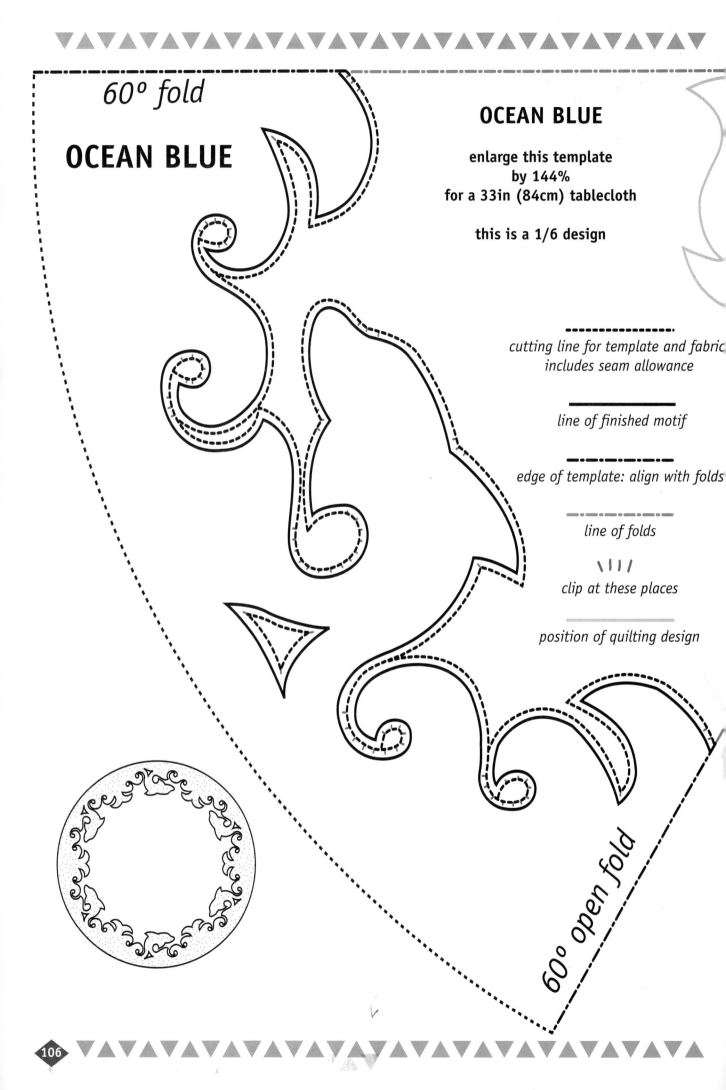

60° fold

OCEAN BLUE

OCEAN BLUE

enlarge this template
by 144%
for a 33in (84cm) tablecloth

this is a 1/6 design

- - - - - - - - - - - - - -
*cutting line for template and fabric
includes seam allowance*

————————
line of finished motif

— - — - — - — - —
edge of template: align with folds

— · — · — · — · —
line of folds

\ | | /
clip at these places

————————
position of quilting design

60° open fold

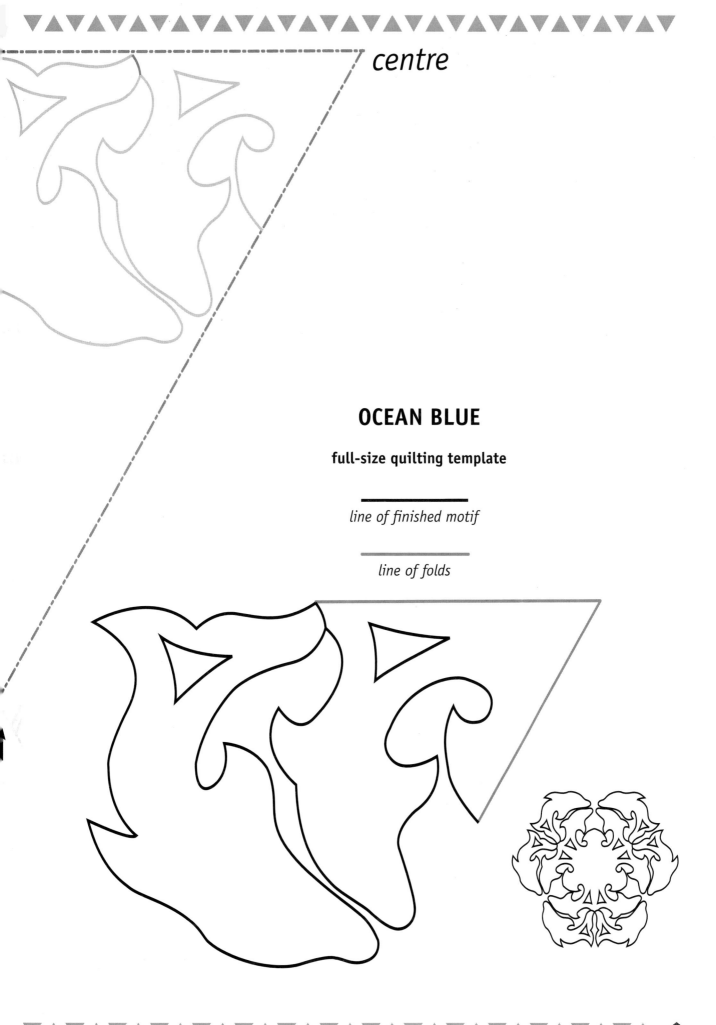

centre

OCEAN BLUE

full-size quilting template

line of finished motif

line of folds

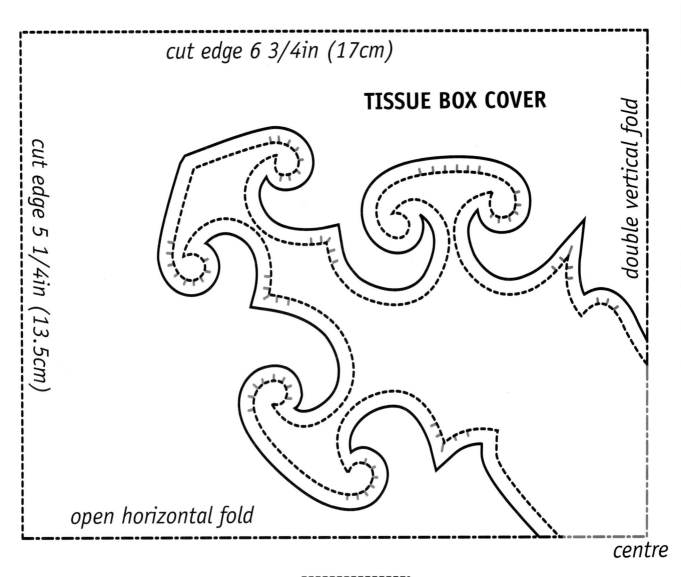

cut edge 6 3/4in (17cm)

TISSUE BOX COVER

double vertical fold

cut edge 5 1/4in (13.5cm)

open horizontal fold

centre

TISSUE BOX COVER

**full-size template
for tissue box cover**

this is a 1/4 design

- - - - - - - - - - - -
*cutting line for template and fabric;
includes seam allowance*

——————
line of finished motif

— · — · — · — · —
edge of template: align with folds

— · · — · · — · · —
line of folds

\ | | /
clip at these places

1/2in (12mm) seam allowance
TISSUE BOX COVER
full-size template
for end panels
(cut 2)
cutting line for template and fabric;
includes seam allowance
line of finished end panel
(bottom line will vary
depending on box size)

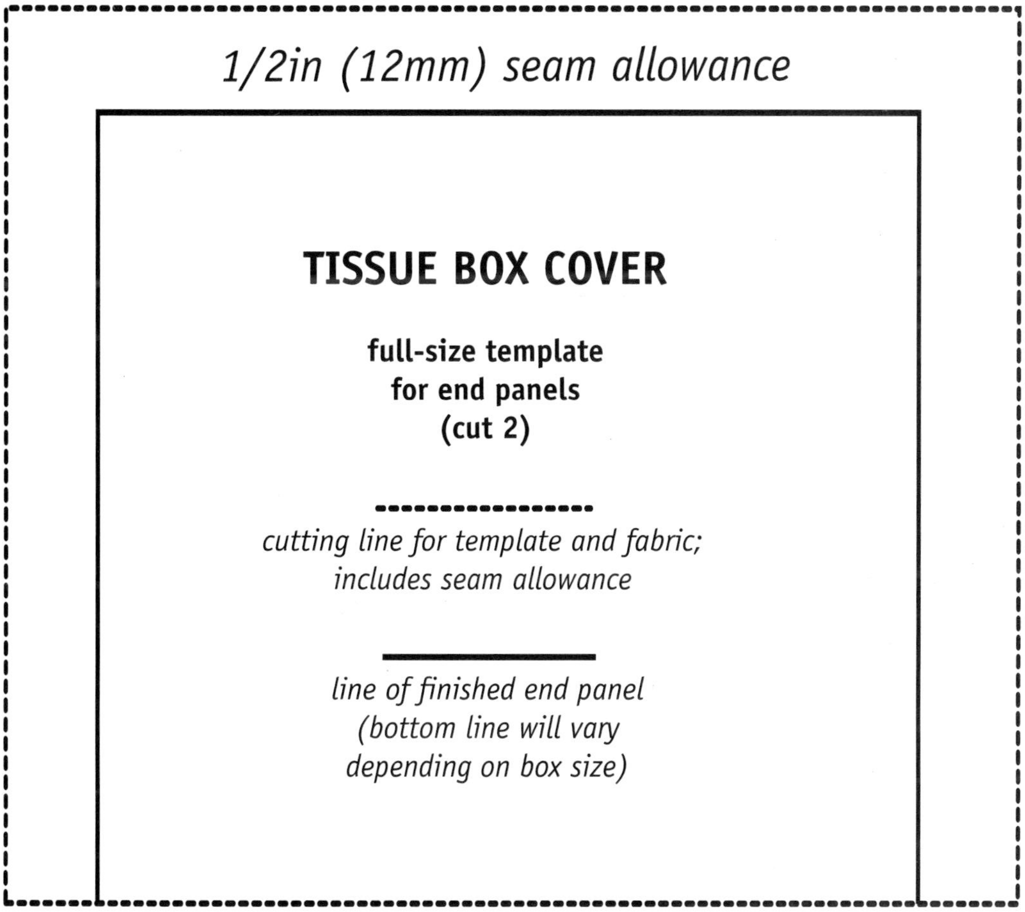

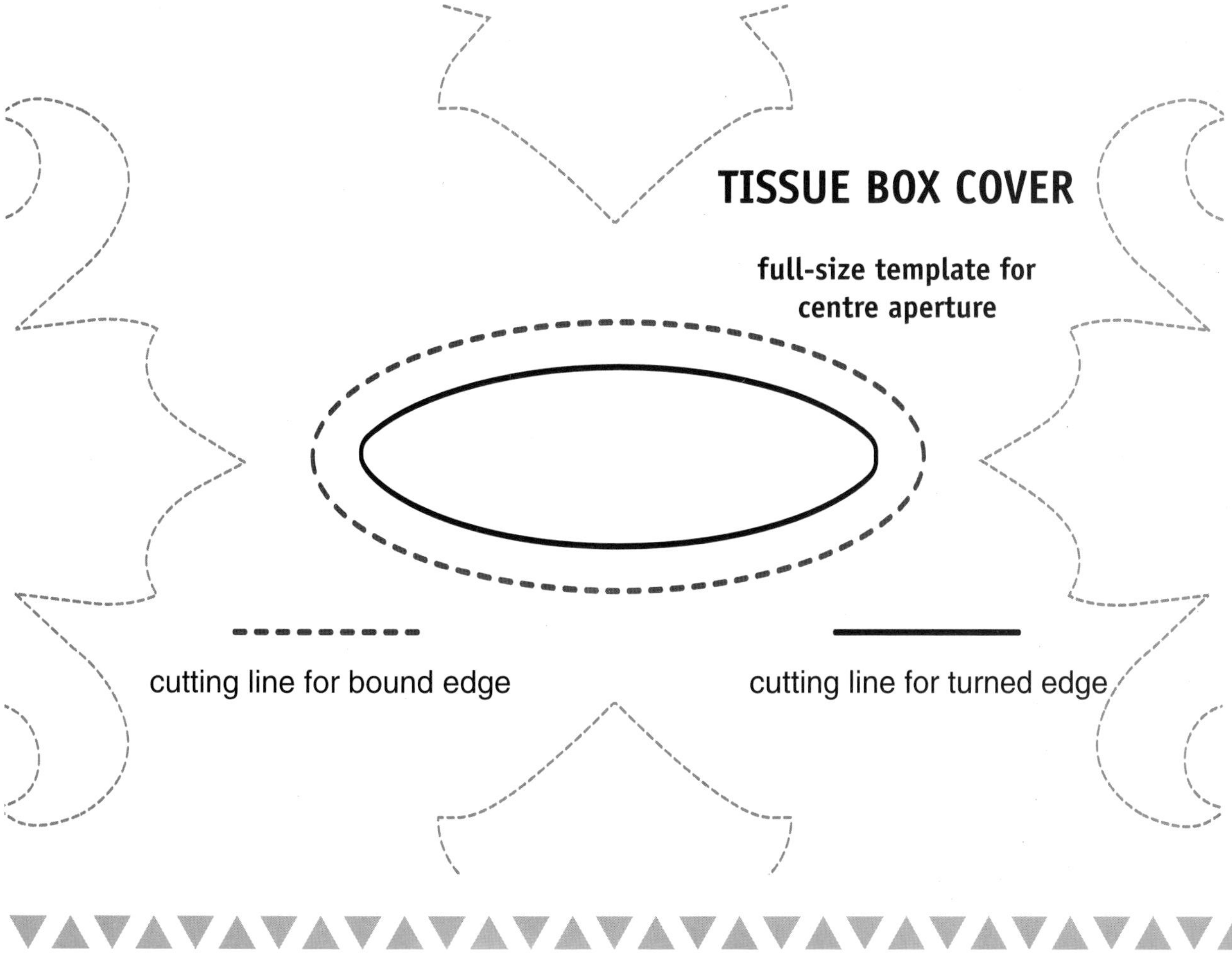

TISSUE BOX COVER
full-size template for
centre aperture
cutting line for bound edge
cutting line for turned edge

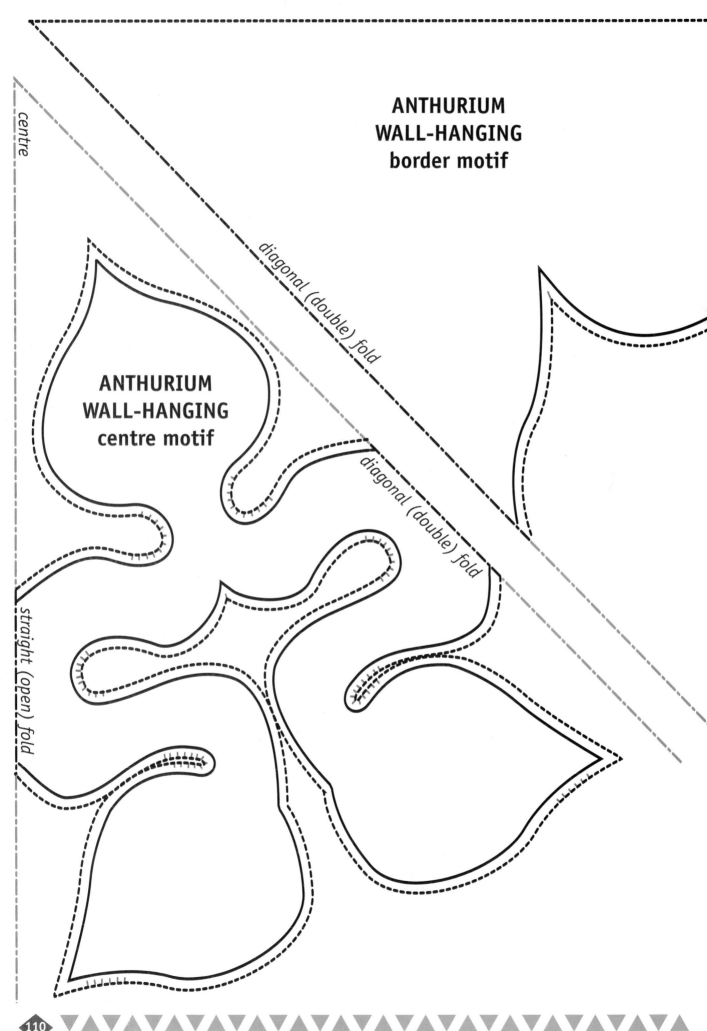

ANTHURIUM
WALL-HANGING
border motif

diagonal (double) fold

diagonal (double) fold

centre

ANTHURIUM
WALL-HANGING
centre motif

straight (open) fold

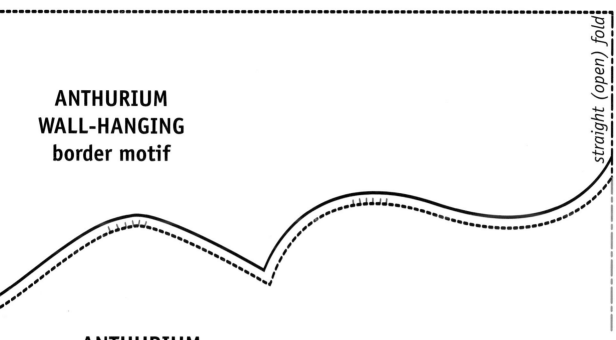

ANTHURIUM
WALL-HANGING
border motif

straight (open) fold

ANTHURIUM
WALL-HANGING

**enlarge templates by 153%
for 43in (109.5cm) wall-hanging;
top straight edge of joined large
template should measure
21 3/4in (55.3cm)**

this is a 1/8 design

· · · · · · · · · · · · · · ·
*cutting line for template and fabric;
includes seam allowance*

───────────
line of finished motif

▬·▬·▬·▬·▬
edge of template: align with folds

▬·▬·▬·▬·▬·▬
line of folds

\ l l /
clip at these places

Resources

BOOKS

Seward, Linda **Patchwork, Quilting, Appliqué**
England: Mitchell Beazley 1987

Kakalia, Kepola **Hawaiian Quilting as an Art**
Honolulu: Deborah U. Kakalia 1976

Shleck, Robert J **The Wilcox Quilts** Hawaii: Lihue
Groves Farm Homestead & Waioli Mission House 1986

Root, Elizabeth **Hawaiian Quilting** Dover
Publications Inc 1989

Faye, Christine & Lovett, Margaret **Kauai Museum
Quilt Collection** Maui: A Kauai Museum Publication
1991

Lucas, Loi **Plants of Old Hawai`i** Hawaii: Bee Press
1982

Jones, Stella M **Hawaiian Quilts** Honolulu: Daughters
of Hawai'i & Honolulu Academy of Arts, and Mission
House Museum Honolulu 1989 revised

Hammond, Joyce D **Tifaifai and Quilting of
Polynesia** Honolulu: University of Hawai`i Press 1986

Singletary, Milly **Hawaiian Quilting Made Easy**
Honolulu: eleventh printing 1994

Duke, Dennis and Harding, Deborah (editors)
America's Glorious Quilts Park Lane, New York
1987; distributed by Crown Publishers Inc, © Hugh
Lauter Associates Inc, New York

VIDEOS

The Hawaiian Quilt A Cherished Tradition; presented
by Hawaii Craftsmen 1986, Honolulu HI
Welcome to my Garden; presented by Sonja 'Konia'
Oberosler 1993, Captain Cook HI

WEBSITES

www.webroots.org/library/usahist/eohvppf0.html
*information on eruptions of Hawaiian volcanoes and
the origins of the islands*

magneticwebdesigns.com/HawaiiHistory/
arrivalofthemissionaries.htm
*Lucy Thurston's account of the missionaries' arrival
in Hawaii*

www.loc.gov/bicentennial/propage/HI/
hi_s_akaka8.html
describes the production of kapa *barkcloth*

www.hulagirlquilts.com/history.html
a brief history of Hawaiian quilting

www.coffeetimes.com/kapa2.htm
more information about kapa *barkcloth*

Suppliers

Fabric

Pauline's Patchwork, Brewers Quay, Hope Square,
Weymouth, Dorset DT4 8TR
tel 01305 766543
website www.paulinespatchwork.co.uk

The Cotton Patch, 1285 Stratford Road, Hall Green,
Birmingham, West Midlands B28 9AJ
tel 0121 702 2840
website www.cottonpatch.co.uk

Quilting frames

R&R Enterprises, 13 Frederick Road,
Malvern Link, Worcs WR14 1RS
tel 01648 563235

Quilting supplies and wadding

Creative Grids (UK) Ltd, Unit 28, Swannington Road,
Broughton Astley, Leics LE9 6TU
tel 0845 450 7722
website www.creativegrids.com

Acknowledgements

*This book is dedicated to my husband Terry,
for his love, support, patience and
encouragement.*

My most sincere thanks to Dinah Travis for agreeing to
write the foreword and introducing me to Hawaiian
Appliqué in 1991. Many thanks to Sue Zane Williams and
Lee Wild for all their help during my visit to Oahu. Also, a
deep debt of gratitude to Lee for agreeing to proofread the
chapter on the history of Hawaiian appliqué and for ensuring
that the Hawaiian spellings are correct. Likewise my most
sincere thanks to Katie Sargent for helping to proofread the
manuscript. Many thanks also to Jane Petty, Gill Rathbone,
Nelleke Kottman, Audrey Critchley and Gill Brennan for
coming to my rescue and quilting the remaining samples as
the deadline drew ever closer. Sincere thanks to Audrey
d'Oliveira and Valerie Lightly for allowing me to photograph
samples of their work for this book, and humble apologies
for not returning their samples earlier! A big thank-you to
my publishers Gail and Christopher Lawther at Teamwork
for their technical support, help and advice throughout this
whole process, and to Rosie Francis for the great
photographs. To Emma and Roger Cooling of Grosvenor
Exhibitions Ltd, thanks for their continuing support to me
and my colleagues in the quilting fraternity. Finally, I'd like
to thank my good friend and colleague Sylvia Critcher for
all her advice, support and encouragement, especially over
the last year.